The Cambridge Introduction to
Tom Stoppard

Tom Stoppard is widely considered to be one of the most important dramatists of contemporary theatre. In this *Introduction*, William Demastes provides an accessible overview of Stoppard's life and work, exploring all the complexity and variety that makes his drama so unique. Illustrated with images from a diverse range of Stoppard productions, the book provides clear evaluations of his major works, including *Rosencrantz and Guildenstern Are Dead*, *Travesties*, *Arcadia*, and *The Coast of Utopia*, to provide the most up-to-date assessment available. Detailed chapters situate each play in the context of its sources, which include Shakespeare and contemporary existential thought, international espionage, quantum physics, chaos theory, romanticism, landscape design, nineteenth-century European intellectual thought, and European totalitarianism. The book also includes a section on Stoppard's Academy Award-winning film *Shakespeare in Love*.

WILLIAM W. DEMASTES is San Diego II Alumni Professor of English at Louisiana State University where he teaches modern theatre and drama.

The Cambridge Introduction to
Tom Stoppard

WILLIAM W. DEMASTES

CAMBRIDGE
UNIVERSITY PRESS

CAMBRIDGE UNIVERSITY PRESS
Cambridge, New York, Melbourne, Madrid, Cape Town,
Singapore, São Paulo, Delhi, Mexico City

Cambridge University Press
The Edinburgh Building, Cambridge CB2 8RU, UK

Published in the United States of America by Cambridge University Press, New York

www.cambridge.org
Information on this title: www.cambridge.org/9781107021952

First published 2012

Printed and bound in the United Kingdom by the MPG Books Group

A catalogue record for this publication is available from the British Library

Library of Congress Cataloging in Publication data
Demastes, William W.
The Cambridge introduction to Tom Stoppard / William Demastes.
    p.   cm. – (Cambridge introductions to literature)
Includes bibliographical references and index.
ISBN 978-1-107-02195-2 (hardback)
1. Stoppard, Tom – Criticism and interpretation.   I. Title.
PR6069.T6Z617   2012
822$'$.914–dc23

                                    2012023160

ISBN 978-1-107-02195-2 Hardback
ISBN 978-1-107-60612-8 Paperback

Contents

Illustrations

Acknowledgements

Support for this book came from several sources. The English Department at Louisiana State University awarded me a Board of Regents Grant, the College of Arts and Sciences granted me a sabbatical, and my Alumni Professorship provided travel and other funds to complete this project. An Andrew W. Mellon Foundation Research Fellowship from the Harry Ransom Center, Austin, TX, allowed me the valuable opportunity to work with the Tom Stoppard Collection, managed so well by that institution.

Vicki Cooper and Fleur Jones at Cambridge University Press were central in getting this project to publication. Jacky Matthews, Rose Cobbe, and Tom Stoppard himself were helpful in ways tangible and intangible. Donald Cooper and Paul Kolnik were invaluable in helping me find photos for this book. I also thank the publishers at Grove Press and Faber & Faber for permission to quote from Stoppard's works. I must also thank a classroom full of "test subjects," dedicated students who helped me figure out which of my bright ideas should be included in or excluded from this text. That noble band included Randon Gilmore, Travis Williams, Anne Grant, Chelsea Demel, Alexandra Clontz, Amanda Lee, Andromeda Love, Tiffany Lyle, Priyanka Mehta, Caroline Newman, Monica Russell, Rebecca Schlicher, and Matthew Stokes. Thanks, everyone.

And, as always, special thanks to Jean and Erin, beacons in my life.

Illustration 1 Tom Stoppard

Introduction: Stoppardianism

I admit it looks odd. The question is does it look odd enough?

The Dog It Was That Died (18)

Mix vaudevillian slapstick with crisp, witty banter. Add a song or two in the style of Gilbert and Sullivan. Try doing a whole scene in limericks. How about a shell game using humans popping in and out of shower stalls? Maybe add some really funny Communist Bloc shenanigans. Set it on a verandah in India, or on a transatlantic passenger liner, or in nineteenth-century Vienna, or in the secret byways of Elsinore Castle. Why not open eyes with a striptease act on a flying trapeze? Maybe parody the work of Agatha Christie. Or play fast and loose with Oscar Wilde. How about tapping into chaos theory or quantum mechanics? How about trying three full-length plays dedicated to the nineteenth-century Russian intelligentsia? Or how about taking on Shakespeare himself? And *always* leave your audiences wondering whether they have just been educated or entertained, in the end allowing for the likelihood of both.

In a nutshell, that is the theatre of Tom Stoppard.[1]

Stoppard has been going strong since the 1960s, generating five decades of consistently good theatre throughout. Consider his breakthrough *Rosencrantz and Guildenstern Are Dead* (1966), an award-winning "first" play that has hardly seen a day since its premiere when it was not being performed somewhere in the world. It was followed by the 1970s masterpieces *Jumpers* (1972) and *Travesties* (1974), which, combined with *Rosencrantz and Guildenstern Are Dead*, would by themselves have been sufficient to rate Stoppard a major playwright. But Stoppard continued, generating two successful West End plays in *Night and Day* (1978) and *The Real Thing* (1982). *Hapgood* (1988) followed, a robust and intellectually challenging "science play," which preceded what many think may be Stoppard's masterpiece, the science-informed, time-warping love story with a twist, *Arcadia* (1995). Stoppard followed that success with *Indian Ink* (1995) and *The Invention of Love* (1997), two more award-winning stage triumphs. This was

1

followed up with yet another wonder of the theatre, his epic trilogy *The Coast of Utopia* (2002), which was in turn followed up with *Rock'n'Roll* (2006).

This extensive list, impressive by itself, fails to include Stoppard's numerous radio plays (like *Albert's Bridge*, 1967), shorter works (like *The Real Inspector Hound*, 1968), television plays (like *Squaring the Circle*, 1984), adaptations (like *On the Razzle*, 1981), and collaborations (like *Every Good Boy Deserves Favor*, 1977). And it overlooks Stoppard's notable dalliance with cinema, writing or co-writing the Oscar-nominated *Brazil* (1985), Oscar-winning *Shakespeare in Love* (1997), and numerous other works, including *The Romantic Englishwoman* (1975), *Despair* (1979), *Empire of the Sun* (1987), *Billy Bathgate* (1991), and *The Russia House* (1991). And then there is his much underappreciated novel, *Lord Malquist and Mr. Moon* (1966).

Anyone who has come in contact with any of the above works will surely agree that Stoppard is a consummate entertainer. But the entertainment is always enriched with an element of intellectual probing that challenges audiences in ways unique to his theatre. When at his best, Stoppard manages to draw from the minimalist likes of Samuel Beckett while making sure our eyes and ears are treated to sights and sounds that at times rival even Disney Productions, Inc. In a 1977 interview, Stoppard laid out his goals: "I want to demonstrate that I can make serious points by flinging a custard pie around the stage for a couple of hours."[2] Though he has yet to work with custard pies, he has tried just about everything else. If the audience is bored, Stoppard has failed. If the audience is not thinking, Stoppard has failed. Stoppard persistently repeats the point whenever interviewed: "Theatre is first and foremost a recreation. But it is not just a children's playground; it can be recreation for people who like to stretch their minds."[3]

Tom Stoppard likes to tell a story about a neighbor who owned a peacock.[4] One morning while drinking coffee and getting ready for work, the neighbor notices that the bird has gotten out of his yard. He puts on his slippers, grabs his coffee, and goes after the peacock, tracking it down on the other side of a major highway full of rush-hour traffic. He grabs the peacock, calms his squirming, awkward burden as best he can, and returns to the highway ready to cross when he feels his loose-fitting pajama pants slipping to his knees. Here is a question: what are the motorists thinking as they speed by a man in pajamas holding a coffee mug and a peacock? What would *you* be thinking?

Glimpses, vignettes, incomplete pictures. Something far less than the whole story. For Stoppard this tale does much to capture the human condition. We all want to know the whole story, to see the big picture, but all we get is a limited view of what is going on. Stoppard's theatre reminds us of the myopia that is so frustratingly central to being human. But his theatre does not sink to pensive self-pity in the standard way that so much modern theatre (and so much art in general) does. Other artists often take this limited drive-by vision and claim that this is all there is to life, concluding that the human condition is basically incomprehensibly absurd. What Stoppard suggests, however, is that our general bewilderment is not the result of a meaningless universe but the result of our current perceptual and intellectual shortcomings as human beings. For Stoppard, it is the great pleasure of life to work at getting a better view and arriving at a better understanding of those great perplexing mysteries of life. C. W. E. Bigsby observes that while the big picture may in fact forever lie just beyond our grasp, maintaining an "irrepressible vitality and eccentric persistence" constitutes "what Stoppard feels to be an authentic response to existence."[5]

One man's bag is nearly empty, and another's is nearly full. They are tossing coins, and for some time now each toss has come up "heads." It is a highly improbable event, but it is not impossible. This is the subject of the opening scene of Stoppard's first big success, *Rosencrantz and Guildenstern Are Dead*. That scene introduces us to what Stoppard will be doing for the next forty-plus years. He will take cold cool logic and just about every sensible way of looking at the world, and he will turn it all on its head over and over again. But Stoppard does not do this merely to entertain us with eccentric portrayals of comically absurd consequences. He focuses on the extreme horizons of probability in order to reveal to us that the world is far stranger and far more interesting than many of us ever imagined.

Stoppard's unique brand of theatre has led to the coining of the word "Stoppardian," putting him among the ranks of modernist and contemporary theatre innovators like Shaw (Shavian), Beckett (Beckettian), and Pinter (Pinteresque). Stoppardianism combines perplexing but undoubted rationalism with baroque linguistic precision to create comic plots filled with paradoxical uncertainties that somehow generate complex but logically satisfying results. Furthermore Stoppard's theatre integrates challenging intellectual concepts with high theatricality, so that, for example, an acrobatics routine becomes an illustration of agile minds at work; creating a deceptively realistic play-within-a-play rocks our notion of what is "the real thing" in theatre or anywhere else; and having one character morph into two characters gives us the chance to think about the multiple roles we all play in real life. Using the entertaining illusion of theatre to reflect upon the serious matters of life – that is Stoppardianism.

Not surprisingly, then, Stoppard takes a stand curiously atypical of many word-bound playwrights. Stoppard, a man who creates play*scripts*, insists that dramatic works are poor shadows of themselves when viewed as stand-alone art. They are best experienced when they take to the stage. Using a production of *Hapgood* as his example, Stoppard observes: "On to a shadowy empty stage, while short-wave radio voices are occupied in keeping tabs on a car somewhere in the streets of London, a swimming-pool's diving tower descends soundlessly from the flies ... the tower comes to earth as lightly as a leaf, and thus with perfect elegance and economy makes the first clear statement of the evening: 'We are at the pool, and now we begin.'" He concludes: "you can't *write* anything that good; and when you think about it, some, perhaps, most, of the best moments you can remember from plays are moments which nobody wrote."[6]

Tom Stoppard energetically recognizes the collaborative nature of the theatre and gives credit where it is due. While his plays are very good reads, they make for even better theatre when placed in the hands of talented theatre practitioners.

The Cambridge Introduction to Tom Stoppard is designed to help the theatregoer, reader, and student to better appreciate the world of Tom Stoppard on the page as well as stage. What immediately follows are a professional chronology, biographical sketch, and chapter on the keys to Stoppard's theatre in general. The subsequent chapters touch upon notable minor works while concentrating on Stoppard's major accomplishments. Interconnections among his works abound, and so it is unfortunate that space limitations prevent discussions of most of Stoppard's cinematic accomplishments (*Shakespeare in Love* is one exception).[7] Generally speaking, though, this book's ultimate goal is to encourage you to see, read, and listen to all of Stoppard's works, even those not covered in these pages.

Professional chronology

A scrap of knowledge to add to our stock.

The Invention of Love (38)

1960

- *The Gamblers* and *A Walk on the Water* are written.

1963

- *A Walk on the Water* is rewritten as a 90-minute television play and broadcast by Rediffusion, November.

1964

- *The Dissolution of Dominic Boot*, a 15-minute radio play, airs in the BBC series *Just Before Midnight*, February.
- *"M" is for Moon among Other Things*, a 15-minute radio play, airs in the BBC series *Just Before Midnight*, April.
- *A Walk on the Water* is Stoppard's first fully staged play, June 30, in Hamburg, Germany, as a translated work entitled *Der Spleen des George Riley*.

1965

- *The Gamblers* is produced at the Bristol Old Vic Theatre School by a Bristol University student group.

1966

- *If You're Glad I'll be Frank*, a radio play, is broadcast by BBC's Third Programme, February 8, on the program *Strange Occupations*.
- *A Separate Peace*, a 30-minute television play, airs on BBC 2, August.
- *Rosencrantz and Guildenstern Are Dead* premieres in Cranston Street Hall at the Edinburgh Festival Fringe, August 24, by the Oxford Theatre Group.
- *Lord Malquist and Mr. Moon* (novel) is published by Faber & Faber.

1967

- *Teeth*, a 30-minute television play, airs February 7.
- *Another Moon Called Earth*, a 30-minute television play, airs in June.
- *Albert's Bridge*, a radio play, airs on BBC's Third Programme, July 13, winning the Prix Italia Award.
- *Rosencrantz and Guildenstern Are Dead* professionally premieres at the Old Vic Theatre, London, April 11, by the National Theatre, directed by Derek Goldby. Stoppard wins the John Whiting Award (with Wole Soyinka), *Plays and Players* Best Play Award, and *Evening Standard* Award for Most Promising Playwright (with David Storey). New York premiere is at the Alvin Theatre, October 16, winning the Tony Award and Drama Critics' Circle Award for Best Play.

1968

- *Enter a Free Man*, originally *A Walk on the Water*, opens at St Martin's Theatre, London, on March 28.
- *The Real Inspector Hound*, a one-act play, opens at the Criterion Theatre, London, on June 17.
- *Neutral Ground*, a television play written in 1965, airs on Thames Television in December.

1969

- *Albert's Bridge* is converted to a stage production and performed by the Oxford Theatre Group in Edinburgh.

1970

- *Where Are They Now?*, a 35-minute radio play, airs January 28 on BBC's Schools Radio.
- *The Dissolution of Dominic Boot*, converted to the mini-film *The Engagement*, airs on American television and in British cinemas.
- *After Magritte*, a one-act play, premieres April 9.

1972

- *Jumpers* premieres February 2 at the Old Vic, London, by the National Theatre, directed by Peter Wood, winning the *Evening Standard* and *Plays and Players* Best Play awards.
- *The Real Inspector Hound* opens in New York and London with *After Magritte* as a curtain-raiser.
- *Artist Descending a Staircase*, a radio play, airs on BBC 3, November 14.

1974

- *Travesties* premieres in London at the Aldwych Theatre by the Royal Shakespeare Company on June 10, winning the *Evening Standard* Award for Best Comedy.
- *Jumpers* opens in New York.
- *Enter a Free Man* opens in New York.

1975

- *Travesties* opens in New York, winning the Tony Award and Drama Critics' Circle Award.
- *Three Men in a Boat*, an adaptation of a Jerome K. Jerome novel, airs on BBC on December 15.
- *The Romantic Englishwoman* (film, with Thomas Wiseman) released.

1976

- *Jumpers* is revived at the Lyttelton Theatre, National Theatre (London).

- *Dirty Linen* and *New-Found-Land,* two one-acts, open as an Ambiance Lunch-Hour Theatre Club Presentation at Inter-Action's Almost Free Theatre, London, April 6. On June 16, the plays transfer to the Arts Theatre, London.

1977

- *Every Good Boy Deserves Favor,* music by André Previn, is given a single performance as part of the Queen's Silver Jubilee at London's Royal Festival Hall on July 1. It is revived with chamber orchestra in London's West End.
- *Professional Foul,* a television play, airs on BBC on September 24, winning the British Critics' Award for best television drama.

1978

- Stoppard is appointed CBE (Commander of the British Empire).
- *Every Good Boy Deserves Favor* opens in Washington, DC.
- *Night and Day* premieres November 8 at London's Phoenix Theatre, winning the *Evening Standard* Award for Best Play.
- *Despair* (film, from a Nabokov novel) released.

1979

- *Every Good Boy Deserves Favor* opens in New York.
- *Undiscovered Country,* an adaptation, premieres at the National Theatre, London, June 20, directed by Peter Wood.
- *Dogg's Hamlet, Cahoot's Macbeth,* two one-act plays, are staged at the Arts Centre of the University of Warwick, Coventry, May 21. On July 30, the plays open at the Collegiate Theatre, London.
- *Night and Day* opens in New York in November 1979.

1980

- *The Human Factor* (film, from Graham Greene's novel) released.

1981

- *On the Razzle*, an adaptation, opens September 1 at the Royal Lyceum Theatre, Edinburgh, as part of the Edinburgh International Festival. It premieres in London at the Lyttelton Theatre, National Theatre, on September 22, directed by Peter Wood.

1982

- *The Real Thing* opens at London's Strand Theatre in November, winning the *Evening Standard* Award for Best Play.
- *The Dog It Was That Died*, a radio play, airs on BBC Radio 4 on December 9.

1984

- *The Real Thing* premieres in New York January 5, at the Plymouth Theater, winning the Tony Award for Best Play, the New York Critics' Award for Best Foreign Play, and the Drama Desk and Outer Circle awards.
- *Squaring the Circle, Poland 1980–81* is televised May on TVS.
- *Rough Crossing*, an adaptation, premieres at the Lyttelton Theatre, National Theatre, October 30.

1985

- *Jumpers* is revived at the Aldwych Theatre, London.
- *The Real Inspector Hound* receives a London revival September 12, at the National Theatre, directed by Tom Stoppard.
- *Brazil* (film, with Terry Gilliam and Charles Mckeown) released, nominated for Academy Award, Best Original Screenplay.

1986

- *Dalliance*, an adaptation of a Schnitzler play, opens at the Lyttelton Theatre, National Theatre, May 27, directed by Peter Wood.
- *Largo Desolato*, an adaptation of a Havel play, opens in Bristol.

1987

- *Empire of the Sun* (film, from J. G. Ballard's novel) released.

1988

- *Hapgood* premieres at the Aldwych Theatre, London, March 8.
- *Artist Descending a Staircase* is revised and given its first stage production.

1989

- *The Dog It Was That Died* is adapted for television and airs January.
- *Hapgood* has US premiere in Los Angeles at the Doolittle Theatre, April 12.

1990

- *Rosencrantz and Guildenstern Are Dead* (film) released.
- *The Russia House* (film, from John le Carré's novel) released.

1991

- *In the Native State*, a radio play, airs on BBC Radio 3 on April 21, winning the Giles Cooper Award.
- *Billy Bathgate* (film, from E. L. Doctorow's novel) released.

1992

- *The Real Inspector Hound* receives New York revival.
- *Shakespeare in Love* (film, with Marc Norman from Norman's original screenplay) released, winning Academy Award for Best Original Screenplay.

1993

- *Arcadia* opens at the Lyttelton Theatre, National Theatre, London, on April 13, directed by Trevor Nunn, winning the *Evening Standard* Best Play of the Year Award and Lawrence Olivier/BBC Award for Best New Play.
- *Travesties* receives a London revival.

1994

- *Hapgood* has New York premiere at the Mitzi E. Newhouse Theater, Lincoln Center, November 11.

1995

- *Indian Ink* premieres at the Aldwych Theatre, London, February 27.
- *Arcadia* premiere in New York at the Vivian Beaumont Theater, Lincoln Center, August 23, winning the Drama Critics' Circle Award.
- *Rosencrantz and Guildenstern Are Dead* revived at Lyttelton Theatre, National Theatre, directed by Matthew Francis, December 14.

1997

- Tom Stoppard is knighted.
- *The Seagull*, Stoppard's version of Chekhov's play, opens May at London's Old Vic.
- *The Invention of Love* opens at the Cottesloe Theatre, National Theatre, London, September 25, directed by Richard Eyre, winning the *Evening Standard* Award for Best Play.

1998

- *Arcadia* is produced in Paris at the Comédie-Française, making Stoppard the first living, non-French playwright produced at that venue.
- *Poodle Springs* (film, from Raymond Chandler and Robert Parker's novel) released.

1999

- *Indian Ink* receives its US premiere at the American Conservatory Theater, San Francisco, February 24.
- *The Real Thing* is revived in London at the Donmar Warehouse, May 27, moving to the Albery Theatre, January 13, 2000.

2000

- *The Invention of Love* has its US premiere in San Francisco at the American Conservatory Theater, January 14.
- *The Real Thing* is revived in New York at the Ethel Barrymore Theater, April 17.

2001

- *The Invention of Love* has its New York premiere, March 29.
- *The Seagull* opens in New York, August 12, at the Delacorte Theatre, Central Park.
- *Enigma* (film, from Robert Harris's novel) released.

2002

- *The Coast of Utopia. Part One: Voyage; Part Two: Shipwreck; Part Three: Salvage* opens at the Olivier Auditorium of the National Theatre, London, during the 2002 season: *Voyage* opens June 27; *Shipwreck* opens July 8; *Salvage* opens July 19. Directed by Trevor Nunn.

2003

- *Jumpers* revived at the Lyttelton Theatre, National Theatre, June 19, directed by David Leveaux.

2004

- *Pirandello's Henry IV*, a version by Stoppard, premieres at the Donmar Warehouse, London, April 29.

2006

- *Rock'n'Roll* opens June 3 at the Jerwood Theatre Downstairs, Royal Court Theatre, London. It moves to the Duke of York Theatre, July 22.
- *The Coast of Utopia. Part One: Voyage; Part Two: Shipwreck; Part Three: Salvage* premieres in New York at the Vivian Beaumont Theater, Lincoln Center: *Voyage* opens November 27; *Shipwreck* opens December 21; *Salvage* opens February 15, 2007. It wins the Tony Award for Best Play.

2007

- *Rock'n'Roll* premieres in New York at the Bernard B. Jacobs Theatre, November 4.

2008

- *Ivanov* by Chekhov, a new version by Stoppard, premieres August 17, Donmar West End at Wyndham's Theatre, London.
- Stoppard is awarded the 2007 Critics' Circle Award for Distinguished Service to the Arts.

2009

- *Arcadia* is revived at the Duke of York Theatre, London, May 27.
- *Every Good Boy Deserves Favor* revived at the National Theatre, January 12, directed by Felix Barrett and Tom Morris. Returned January 9 to February 17, 2010.
- New version of Checkhov's *The Cherry Orchard* for Sam Mendes and Neal Street Productions opens in New York, January 3.

2010

- *The Real Thing* is revived at London's Old Vic Theatre, April.

2011

- *Arcadia* is revived at the Ethel Barrymore Theater, New York, March 17.
- *Rosencrantz and Guildenstern Are Dead* is revived at Chichester Festival Theatre, May 20; moves to Royal Haymarket Theatre, June 22.

2012

- Film adaptation of Leo Tolstoy's *Anna Karenina* is scheduled for release.
- *Parade's End*, a five-part television adaptation based on Ford Madox Ford's novel, is scheduled for release by BBC 2 and HBO.

Chapter 1

Stoppard: briefly, a life in the theatre

Biography is the worst possible excuse for getting people wrong.

Indian Ink (5)

Art cannot be subordinate to its subject, otherwise it is not art but biography, and biography is the mesh through which our real life escapes.   *The Invention of Love* (93)

Many biographers, critics, and analysts have made much of Stoppard's status as an outsider who, many claim, ultimately became more English than native-born citizens. His life as an outsider almost certainly has had an impact on his vision of the world as well as on his art, but how much of an impact is a matter of pure conjecture. Asked in 1998 about possible autobiographical elements in his work, Stoppard observed, "the area in which I feed off myself is really much more to do with thoughts I have had rather than days I have lived."[1] What is absolutely certain is that Stoppard has led a full and memorable life.

Tom Stoppard was born Tomas Straussler[2] (nicknamed Tomik) on July 3, 1937 in Zlín, Czechoslovakia, the second son of Dr. Eugene Straussler and Martha Beckova Straussler. Tom's father was a physician employed by Bata, a large shoe manufacturer world-renowned for its progressive, employee-friendly management style. In 1939, when World War II seemed imminent, Bata moved the Strausslers (and many other employees of Jewish descent) to its Singapore operation in order for them to escape Nazi persecution. The move, however, only changed the face of the enemy for the Strausslers. As Singapore fell to the Japanese in 1941, Tom's family became refugees once again, and, first sailing toward Australia, their ship changed course and found its way to India. Tom's father was delayed in his escape and went missing during the turmoil of Singapore's fall. Years later he was reported to have died when the Japanese sank the ship he was on.

Tom spent the war years in Darjeeling, India, where his mother managed a Bata shoe shop and where he attended a multiracial, American-run school. He loved the colonial grandeur of India, was attracted to most things English, and became a fan of American culture as a result of meeting American soldiers while in Darjeeling. In 1946, Tom's mother married Kenneth Stoppard, a British officer stationed in India, who returned with his new family after the war to England to become a machine-tools salesman. The Strausslers all became Stoppards and turned to the business of becoming English, with Tom's mother doing her best to erase the memory of their Eastern European roots in the interest of having her children finally fit in. Tom was only occasionally curious enough to ask his mother about their past and was rarely able to get much information from her about relatives on the continent or about his possible Jewish heritage. Tom was not one to resist his mother's efforts to have them fit in, though somehow his vaguely noticeable accent has never quite disappeared.

Tom started his English education in a Nottinghamshire prep school but soon transferred to Pocklington School in Yorkshire with his older brother, Peter. Tom was a good student who also loved sports, especially cricket. He read widely and fell particularly in love with American writers like Hemingway and Steinbeck. He was good at Latin and might have become a classics student had he gone to college. However, bored by the pace and general tedium of classroom life, in 1954 Tom Stoppard left school at age 17 to make his way as a journalist, dreaming of some day forging a career as an international reporter. He worked in Bristol for the *Western Daily Press* and then the *Bristol Evening World*. He loved being out in the world seeing firsthand how it operated, and he made himself known about town by wearing a faddish trilby hat and slightly oversized raincoat. He scraped out a living reporting on local events, writing humorous columns, and occasionally filling in as theatre reviewer. Never completely comfortable merely reporting just the facts, and frankly bored by being required to do just that, he frequently skipped out to the cinema and returned to his assignment in time to gather essential information, fabricating much of the rest. On occasion he would invent man-on-the-street interviews and pass them off as authentic. Lengthy article titles provide a taste of Stoppard's style: "British actors with real drawing power in the States can more or less be counted on one paw of a two-toed sloth"; "Tom Stoppard treads THE BEATNIK TRACK to find a roomful of people all acting as if they were alone."

Eventually he was drawn to and formally assigned the Bristol theatre scene. Theatre in Britain during the late 1950s and early 1960s was a tantalizing thing for a writer with a flair for the dramatic. Playwright John Osborne and other "angry young men" who followed him were flanked by Samuel Beckett's minimalist revolution in the theatre, which ran side-by-side with visually mesmerizing theatre work done by the likes of directors Peter Brook and Peter Hall. While in Bristol, Stoppard saw excellent theatre at the Bristol Old Vic, including the work of rising star Peter O'Toole, who in one season played both Hamlet and Jimmy Porter from Osborne's ground-breaking *Look Back in Anger*.

While making a living as a journalist, Stoppard caught the playwriting fever and wrote *A Walk on the Water* (1960), which would eventually become *Enter a Free Man*. While waiting for word on the play's fate from various theatre managers, Stoppard put together the beginnings of several other plays. Eventually, thanks to his new (and soon-to-become lifelong) agent Kenneth Ewing, he received a £100 advance from the H. M. Tennents producing agency, though the option ran out without *A Walk on the Water* being produced. Between 1960 and 1962, Stoppard wrote *The Gamblers* (which the BBC briefly considered for production) and *The Stand-Ins* (whose working title was *Murder at Mousetrap Manor* and which would become *The Critics*, which then became *The Real Inspector Hound*). Though his work attracted interest, none of these pieces found its way onto the stage until later in Stoppard's career.

By 1963 Stoppard decided to move to London, in time to experience the swinging youth culture of the most fashionable city in the Western world. Stoppard took to it all with great relish. He began writing for the short-lived *Scene* and befriended his old acquaintance Peter O'Toole (now famous thanks to the film *Lawrence of Arabia*). *A Walk on the Water* was reworked and filmed for television. It aired in November 1963 as a hasty replacement for a show deemed inappropriate following President Kennedy's assassination. Without the time to advertise and given the international distraction that led to the play being aired, Stoppard's first success was hardly noticed.

In 1964 Stoppard succeeded at getting two 15-minute radio plays produced: *The Dissolution of Dominic Boot* (February) and *"M" is for Moon among Other Things* (April). Stoppard also had three short stories published by Faber & Faber in *Introduction 2*, an anthology introducing new writers. And he wrote five episodes for the BBC daily family radio series, *The Dales*. He also completed an unperformed television play, *This Way Out with Samuel Boot*. He was making money as a writer, but he remained basically "for hire" and anonymous to the public.

During this same year Stoppard won a Ford Foundation grant and went to Berlin from May to August, where, along with several other young writers, he was given complete freedom to work on his writing. Focusing on an idea his agent Kenneth Ewing casually suggested, Stoppard began writing a play about two minor attendants from Shakespeare's *Hamlet* who travel to England and meet a mad King Lear. Stoppard wrote several drafts of this work, initially entitling it *Rosencrantz and Guildenstern Meet King Lear*. While in Germany, he managed to get a German translation of *A Walk on the Water* staged in Hamburg, his first full stage production, moderately well received.

In 1965, Stoppard managed to get a revised version of *The Gamblers* staged at Bristol University. He also wrote a series of episodes for *A Student's Diary: An Arab in London*, a radio series that was translated and aired in the Middle East by the Overseas Service. It earned him a secure £20 a week. During the same year Stoppard adapted his short story "The Story" into *A Paragraph for Mr. Blake*, which aired on British television. But most exciting was the fact that the Royal Shakespeare Company took a 12-month option on his still unfinished Rosencrantz and Guildenstern play. Stoppard submitted and edited numerous revisions, but in the end the option expired. However, Stoppard's work was reaching the highest levels of the British theatre world, and that was good reason to hope.

The year 1966 started well enough. In February his radio play *If You're Glad I'll be Frank* aired. Stoppard was also commissioned to revise the script of Slawomir Mrozek's *Tango* for the Royal Shakespeare Company, a clear sign that his talents were being recognized by important theatre people, and his own work *A Separate Peace* was televised. During this busy year, Stoppard further revised what would become *Rosencrantz and Guildenstern Are Dead*, and it was finally performed at the Edinburgh Fringe Festival by the amateur Oxford Theatre Group, where it got mixed reviews but a lot of attention. Ronald Bryden of the *Observer* was one critic who wrote a glowing review,[3] and the play gathered renewed attention in London. This was Stoppard's big break, though he would have to wait a bit longer before he could bask in the fame that this play was about to win him. In the meantime, he had begun to believe that his reputation would be made as a novelist: *Lord Malquist and Mr. Moon* was published in August, the same month as the Edinburgh Fringe Festival performed *Rosencrantz and Guildenstern Are Dead*. Though it certainly deserved a better reception than it received, *Lord Malquist and Mr. Moon* was hardly noticed by the press and sold only 688 initial copies.[4] Stoppard stayed the course as a playwright.

The year 1967 was Stoppard's breakout year. *Teeth* and *Another Moon Called Earth* were televised. But all of this was small change compared to the fact that *Rosencrantz and Guildenstern Are Dead* was professionally staged by Kenneth Tynan and the National Theatre at London's Old Vic Theatre. It was an overwhelming success. Stoppard won numerous best play awards in Britain, and later the New York production won a Tony Award and the Drama Critics' Circle Award for Best Play. In July Stoppard's radio play

Albert's Bridge was aired by the BBC and won the prestigious Prix Italia Award. At long last, Tom Stoppard was an "overnight success."

It seemed that Stoppard's private life was shaping up quite nicely as well. Though this particular episode of domestic bliss was short-lived, interviews at the time suggest a settled home life with wife and children. On March 26, 1965 he married Jose Ingle. On May 4, 1966 their first child, Oliver, was born, and on September 20, 1969 Barnaby was born. During this period, thanks in large part to *Rosencrantz and Guildenstern Are Dead*, Stoppard's star rose meteorically. And thanks to this newfound celebrity, *Enter a Free Man* (formerly *A Walk on the Water*) found its way to the London stage in March 1968. Stoppard thoroughly relished the attention and celebrity, accepting invitations to public events and doing interviews whenever asked. Unfortunately, the many distractions and pressures of fame led to serious marital difficulties by early 1970, though actual divorce proceedings took two years to complete.

During this period, Stoppard produced several minor pieces, but his next major work would not arrive until 1972, leaving critics wondering if Stoppard were something of a one-hit wonder. Among these lesser pieces was *The Real Inspector Hound* (June 1968), an Agathie Christie spoof with a twist. Granada television aired *Neutral Ground*, a spy thriller, in December 1968. In April 1970, *After Magritte* made it as a theatre-club production, eventually double-billing with *The Real Inspector Hound* and reaching the West End in 1972. Also in 1970, *Where are They Now?* aired for BBC Schools Radio, and *The Engagement* (a 45-minute version of *The Dissolution of Dominic Boot*) appeared on American television and in British cinemas. In 1971 Stoppard wrote *Dogg's Our Pet* for the Almost-Free Theatre in Soho, a community theatre founded by his friend, the American expatriate Ed Berman, whose pseudonym, Professor Dogg, inspired the play's title, which is an anagram of Dogg's Troupe. Stoppard also wrote the unproduced screenplay *Galileo*, later converted for the stage but never produced.

Stoppard was clearly keeping busy. But this was not the quality of output expected of a man whom some hoped would breathe new vitality into a flagging British theatre. During this same period Stoppard married Miriam Moore-Robinson on February 11, 1972. Their first child, William, was born on March 7, and Edmund was born on September 16, 1974. With Tom's two previous children (Oliver and Barnaby) living with them, Tom's family life was robust and by all accounts idyllic. Miriam was a successful physician and pharmaceuticals executive who became a self-help author and popular television personality, and the two would become the power couple of the 1970s and 1980s. The marriage would end in 1989.

Fortunes changed shortly after Stoppard's second marriage, including major professional breakthroughs with *Jumpers* (1972) and *Travesties* (1974). Both plays won major critical awards and were very successful at the box office.[5] These works clearly dampened critical concern that Stoppard was a one-hit wonder and went a long way to defining Stoppard's "Stoppardian" style. But critics tended now to express a growing disappointment at the passionlessness of these urbane, witty, intellectually challenging farce-comedies. Added to this complaint was concern that his plays were distinctly non-political and unnervingly comically upbeat. These two qualities ran counter to trends in contemporary British theatre, dominated at the time by the legacy of the angry young playwrights, leftist ideology, and existential sobriety.

In 1975 his first produced screenplay (co-written with Thomas Wiseman, based on Wiseman's novel), *The Romantic Englishwoman*, was released.[6] Stoppard pursued collaboration and adaptation for cinema on numerous future occasions, enjoying the overall enterprise but often being frustrated by diversions and delays that occur throughout the production process. In 1976, Stoppard extended his relationship with Ed Berman and his Inter-Action Theatre by writing *The Dogg's Troupe 15-minute Hamlet*, which was performed on a converted double-decker bus. And on the date of Berman's naturalization as a British citizen, they produced Stoppard's *Dirty Linen* (initially titled *Maddie Sees It Through*) and *New-Found-Land* for the Ambiance Lunch-Hour Theatre Club at the Almost-Free Theatre. The performance package transferred to London's Arts Theatre and was wildly popular.

Taking a turn toward activism in the mid-1970s, Stoppard became a supporter of Eastern Bloc dissidents and actively denounced Soviet totalitarianism. In December 1976, he spoke at a rally in London's Trafalgar Square against Soviet abuse of dissidents, joining in a march to the Soviet Embassy. He was involved with numerous organizations, including the British Writers' Committee for the Release of Soviet Refusnik Authors and Journalists, Writers and Scholars Educational Trust, Index on Censorship, and the British Campaign for the Release of Indonesian Political Prisoners. He visited Moscow and Leningrad in 1977 as part of Amnesty International's "Prisoner of Conscience" campaign for justice. He also returned to Czechoslovakia in June 1977 for the first time since his childhood, meeting the recently released Czech playwright and future president Václav Havel, whose theatre work and political activism Stoppard greatly admired. Out of this contact with these dissident communities, Stoppard wrote *Every Good Boy Deserves Favor* (July 1977) with André Previn (who wrote the music for a full-scale symphony accompaniment) and the TV play *Professional Foul* (September 1977; Stoppard dedicated the play to Havel[7]). Both plays employ Stoppard's now famous wit, but added to that wit is a new and genuine activist angle. Meeting by accident a distant relative in Prague, he also began more seriously to research and acknowledge his Czech and Jewish roots. Stoppard continued his collaboration with Ed Berman during this period. In May 1979 they put on *Dogg's Hamlet, Cahoot's Macbeth* at the University of Warwick, under the auspices of Berman's British American Repertory Company (BARC).

Stoppard's next major play reveals his interest in journalism and matters of free speech. *Night and Day* (1978) was Stoppard's first major play written expressly for a West End venue, specifically for theatre producer Michael Codron, adhering fairly closely to the expectations and conventions of well-made realistic theatre and utilizing a smaller cast than his previous major works (which often included larger casts since the National Theatre and RSC were supported by state subsidies).

During the period from 1978 to 1991, Stoppard added screenwriting to his list of accomplishments. In 1978 Stoppard's screenplay of Nabokov's novel *Despair*, directed by Rainer Werner Fassbinder, was released. Though Stoppard was dissatisfied with the pace of the final product, the film was very successful in Germany and elsewhere. In 1980 *The Human Factor* was released, based on a Graham Greene novel. In 1985, he co-wrote *Brazil* with Terry Gilliam and was nominated for an Academy award. In 1987 his screenplay of J. G. Ballard's novel *Empire of the Sun* was released, during which time he befriended Steven Spielberg, with whom he would work on numerous projects over the next two decades. Throughout this period, Stoppard served as uncredited script doctor and adviser for Spielberg[8] and others on such works as *Restoration, Schindler's List, Hook, Chaplin, Jurassic Park, Indiana Jones and the Last Crusade, Always, Sleepy Hollow,* and *The Bourne Ultimatum*. In 1990 the film of Stoppard's screenplay of John le Carré's *Russia House* (starring Sean Connery) was released, and in the same year he directed his screenplay rewrite of *Rosencrantz and Guildenstern Are Dead*. The finished product won Stoppard the Golden Lion Award at the Venice Film Festival. In 1991 *Billy Bathgate* was released (starring Dustin Hoffman), script by Stoppard, based on E. L. Doctorow's novel. And after numerous delays HBO released *Poodle Springs* in 1998, Stoppard's reworking of a Raymond Chandler story. *Vatel* was released in 2000, followed in 2001 by *Enigma*, based on Robert Harris's novel. While many playwrights accept Hollywood projects for the huge financial gains they generate, and while Stoppard did make a good deal of money working on Hollywood projects, he nonetheless insists (as perhaps few playwrights can) that plays can make as much money as screenplays; they just take a bit longer.[9] He additionally observes that "you can astonish the audience too easily in the movies. It is much more of a challenge to create a 'moment' in the theater."[10] What attracts him to Hollywood are the good writers in the business – the reason for his interest in adaptations – rather than Hollywood per se.

Stoppard was also willing at this time to express public support for newly empowered Conservative prime minister Margaret Thatcher, seeing her as "a subversive influence, which I found very interesting."[11] Her free market endorsements were less than fully embraced by more liberal elements of British culture, placing Stoppard in particular contention with his more liberal theatre colleagues. Perhaps not coincidentally, Stoppard subsequently steered clear of national politics and became more personal in his work.

This more personal work surfaced as another Michael Codron production in the West End. *The Real Thing* (1982) tackles love, infidelity, and commitment. It is curious that during this same period several of Stoppard's contemporaries also wrote plays about matrimonial infidelity, including Peter Nichols's *Passion Play* and Harold Pinter's *Betrayal*. *The Real Thing* was a great success and appears to have led to a movement among critics to "discover" a certain emotional depth in Stoppard's earlier works as well. Maybe the early critical charges that Stoppard was a coldly exacting intellectual playwright had always been something of an overstatement. Or perhaps earlier productions failed to investigate the more intimate dimensions of their respective texts.

During the 1980s Stoppard penned three adaptations while grappling with his next major play. *On the Razzle* (1981) starred Felicity Kendal in a Stoppard play for the first time. It was produced by the National Theatre and is an adaptation of Johann Nestroy's *Einen Jux will er sich machen*, which is also the source for Thornton Wilder's *The Matchmaker* (1954), which itself was adapted into the musical *Hello, Dolly!* (1964). *Rough Crossing* (1984) is based on Ferenc Molnár's farce *Play at the Castle*, which had been adapted by P. G. Wodehouse in 1928 as *The Play's the Thing*, starring Alfred Lunt and Lynn Fontaine. André Previn joined Stoppard once again and provided the music for this adaptation. *Dalliance* (1986), an adaptation of an Arthur Schnitzler melodrama, followed.

In February 1986 Stoppard's political side resurfaced when he organized a daylong roll call at the National Theatre, gathering solid support from a large list of celebrities who were organized to call out the names of the nearly 9,000 Soviet Jews detained in the USSR against their will. Among the many celebrities were Felicity Kendal, Jeremy Irons, Andrew Lloyd Webber, Christopher Fry, Kingsley Amis, and Twiggy.

Stoppard's long-awaited next major work arrived in 1988. *Hapgood*, with Kendal in the title role, is to date Stoppard's least successful major play. It follows Stoppard's earlier interest in writing spy thrillers, but this time he connects espionage with the multiple nature of individual identity and tries to bring everything together by introducing us all to quantum physics. Narratively dense, intellectually challenging, and not all that funny, Stoppard tried on several occasions and at different venues (including Los Angeles and New York) to rework and restage the play but with only limited success.

What followed was Stoppard's most complete work for the theatre. *Arcadia* (1993) combines structural sophistication, intellectual savvy, and emotional depth, which have all surfaced throughout Stoppard's career but never with such balanced effect. Science is a centerpiece once again, this time moving into chaos theory, thermodynamics, plant morphology, and population theory. This may sound distinctly untheatrical, but in Stoppard's hands – and apparently having learned from his experiences with *Hapgood* – the material seems almost naturally made for the theatre. The play won every major award and transferred from the National Theatre to the West End, eventually arriving in New York to equally rave reviews. Its popularity extended quickly to regional and university productions throughout the United States and, in translation, around the world.

Overlapping the smash London success of *Arcadia*, Stoppard adapted his earlier radio play *In the Native State* into *Indian Ink* and in 1994 opened it in the West End even as *Arcadia* was still packing in audiences. It was produced by Michael Codron and starred Felicity Kendal, who moved from her role in *Arcadia* into the lead in *Indian Ink*. This play is a minor gem among Stoppard plays, nostalgic in mood yet decidedly opposed to over-romanticized British colonial excesses.

But Stoppard was not yet done with the 1990s. In September 1997 *The Invention of Love* opened at the National Theatre. It involves an unlikely central character, Cambridge University classics scholar and minor poet A. E. Housman, who is split into two characters onstage, one youthful, the other deceased. This play of intellectualism amid failed pursuits of homoerotic love includes an extended appearance by Oscar Wilde. It won the *Evening Standard* Award for Best Play. Opening in New York on March 29, 2001, its two stars, Richard Easton and Robert Sean Leonard, both won Tony Awards.

If that is not enough, in 1997 Stoppard generated a version of Chekhov's *The Seagull* – Chekhov's most self-consciously "dramatic" major work, an appropriate choice for Stoppard – which included Kendal in London (1997) and

Meryl Streep in New York (2001). And Stoppard was awarded an Oscar in 1998 for co-writing the screenplay for *Shakespeare in Love*. Far less successful during this period was an effort to produce an animated film version of *Cats* with Spielberg and Andrew Lloyd Webber. The project began in early 1994, but after several years involving numerous rewrites, legal difficulties shelved the project in the early 2000s.

In between all this productivity, Stoppard received his knighthood in 1997, and in 2000 the Order of Merit. However, moving gracefully and successfully into his 60s, he was far from retired as a playwright.

In 2002, by far Stoppard's most ambitious project to date premiered, a three-part epic entitled *The Coast of Utopia*. It comprises three major plays, *Part One*: *Voyage*, *Part Two*: *Shipwreck*, and *Part Three*: *Salvage*. This trilogy opened at the Olivier Auditorium of the National Theatre, London, during the 2002 season, to great fanfare and was remounted to great critical acclaim at New York's Lincoln Center in 2006. This massive, far-reaching epic rivals the great nineteenth-century Russian and British novels in ambition and quality, and nearly in length. *Voyage* is set in Tsarist Russia between summer 1833 and autumn 1841. *Shipwreck* is set in Russia, Paris, Dresden, Nice, and elsewhere, from 1846 to 1852. And *Salvage* opens in a wealthy Russian exile's home in Hampstead, England in 1853, ending in June 1862. It is a rich reflection of all that went well – including the emancipation of the serfs – and poorly – including the failed spread of social justice – during this little-remembered but important period in European history. In London and New York, the play was the event of its respective seasons, masterfully blending Stoppardian wit with the leavened wisdom of an artist who has experienced his own pretty fair share of life's ups and downs.

In 2006, Stoppard staged yet another play, far more modest in scope and scale but intriguing in its own way. *Rock'n'Roll* centers around Czechoslovakia's 1989 Velvet Revolution and brings to the stage material that seems to have been gathering in Stoppard's consciousness for some years. It opened on June 3, 2006 at the Royal Court Theatre, London, directed by Trevor Nunn. It is alternatingly set in Cambridge, England and Prague, Czechoslovakia from 1968 to 1990. Central is a Stoppardian complaint, seen in *The Coast of Utopia* and elsewhere, that idealism leads to revolution which eventually devolves from grandiose dreams to petty self-interest. Given the leftist political leanings of the Royal Court Theatre and considering Stoppard's generally right-leaning inclination, the fact that the Royal Court included Stoppard's play in its fiftieth anniversary season was mildly controversial. Perhaps, however, Stoppard's stature raises him above such concerns.

In 2008 he was awarded the 2007 Critics' Circle Award for Distinguished Service to the Arts. And on May 19, 2008 Stoppard was among seven recipients of the Dan David Prize. The award recognizes unique impacts on the world by its awardees and is extended by Tel Aviv University in Israel. Israeli president Shimon Peres gave the keynote address and distributed the million dollar award among the awardees. Stoppard was recognized for "his portrayal of the search for meaning while displaying dazzling theatricality and genius for laughter." Along with Stoppard, award recipients for 2008 included Al Gore. Stoppard – Holocaust refugee and exiled Jew – must surely have appreciated this award. One can only wonder if in his mind it rivals his British knighthood. The Dan David Prize and British knighthood in their respective ways recognize a man whose one-of-a-kind blend of so many qualities marks him as truly unique.

Sir Tom Stoppard currently lives in London. A good deal of his time is spent overseeing the many worldwide revivals of his plays, including a 2009 London revival of *Arcadia* with his actor son Ed Stoppard playing Valentine. However, once again, speculation about retirement has proven premature. In 2012, Stoppard's film adaptation of Leo Tolstoy's *Anna Karenina*, and *Parade's End*, his five-part television adaptation based on Ford Madox Ford's novel, are scheduled for release.

Chapter 2

Keys to Stoppard's theatre

> I'm just showing that the facts would fit more than one set of possibilities.   *The Dog It Was That Died* (23)

On several occasions, Stoppard shares a story about an outdoor production of Shakespeare's *Tempest* set in a garden before a small lake. When it came for Ariel to make an exit, the sprite, by miracle of theatre, flitted across the lake's surface, making the lightest of splashes until out of sight. The completely forgettable stage direction "Exit Ariel" became a truly magical happening thanks to the theatrical ingenuity of constructing a small walkway just inches under the lake's surface. Stoppard retells this story with some frequency to draw the distinction between "drama" and "theatre"[1] and to emphasize that he is forever aware of the fact that the drama he writes is a text meant to be staged as "theatre."

What we get from Stoppard are opportunities for events much like Ariel magically flitting over enchanted waters. The fact that Stoppard's plays are so entertainingly playful and engagingly witty has frequently left critics wondering whether Stoppard is or should be considered a serious playwright. John Gardner captures this concern in his 1978 work, *On Moral Fiction*: "the tone, the ultra-theatrical pizzazz, the delightfully flashy language which is Stoppard's special gift – all these warn us in advance that the treatment of ideas is likely to be more fashionable than earnest-predictable talk about the meaninglessness of things, the impossibility of 'knowing,' and so on."[2] Gardner is correct in seeing Stoppard swimming against the current of contemporary "serious" theatre in that Stoppard does avoid "earnest-predictable" visions of contemporary life. And as Gardner implies, Stoppard's "pizzazz" may make him appear to be little more than an urbane upper-middle-class wit determined to curry the favor of the well-to-do with his cocktail-party philosophies. But as Gardner also implies, Stoppard does show an awareness of the angst that permeates modern Western society; it is just that he is not terribly interested in "earnest-predictable" expressions of dour existentialism. Some have seen Stoppard as someone who has chosen to crash through the despair and move on with life, an interpretation that has resulted in these same critics labeling Stoppard a post-absurdist.[3]

The theatre of the absurd[4] and existential philosophy in general promote the idea that the world is utterly meaningless and so the pursuit of meaning is nothing but a fool's errand. For Stoppard, however, there is a persistent belief that meaning*ful*ness exists and that there is a governing force of some sort that organizes the universe. The problem is – recalling the peacock on the roadside – humanity is still far short of being able to put together the whole picture. Much like the absurdists, Stoppard's vision concedes we see a world that *appears* disjointed and random. But for Stoppard appearance and actuality are not the same thing, leaving a lingering hope that there is an organizing principle – even perhaps a god – that simply has escaped our vision up to this point.

Stoppard's theatre involves testing premises, premonitions, intuitions about how the world works. And in a world where certainty seems unattainable, plausibility is what Stoppard pursues. Consider the following observation by Stoppard:

> They found traces of amino acid in volcanic rock – the beginnings
> of life. Now a straight line of evolution from amino acid in volcanic
> rock all the way through to Shakespeare's sonnets – that strikes me
> as possible, but a very long shot. Why back such an outsider?
> However preposterous the idea of God is, it seems to have an
> edge in plausibility.[5]

This is not to say that Stoppard is rejecting Darwin in favor of traditional theology. Rather, Stoppard invests time and energy pursuing any number of plausibilities among a world of options and opportunities, testing their viability and confronting their limitations.

While Stoppard may personally lean toward one alternative over another, he rarely shows his hand onstage. In point of fact, Stoppard confesses, "I write

plays because dialogue is the only respectable way of contradicting yourself."[6]
So in his theatre, options are presented and audiences are invited to consider, debate, and select. Stoppard himself famously observes of his theatre:

> there is very often *no* single, clear statement in my plays. What there is, is a series of conflicting statements made by conflicting characters, and they tend to play a sort of infinite leap-frog. You know, an argument, a refutation, then a rebuttal of the refutation, then a counter-rebuttal, so that there is never any point in this intellectual leap-frog at which I feel *that* is the speech to stop it on, that is the last word.[7]

This point is echoed in Kenneth Tynan's recollection that Stoppard "once said that his favorite line in modern English drama came from [Christopher Hampton's] *The Philanthropist*: 'I'm a man of no convictions – at least, I *think* I am.'"[8] As far as Stoppard the playwright is concerned, the point certainly applies.

Argue, refute, refute the refutation. Confessing onstage that he "doesn't know," that he does not have the answer to life's persistent questions, frustrates some theatregoers. But that he longs for a ceiling view of the situation – for a good reason why the man is carrying a peacock – is what gives Stoppard's plays their complex richness and vitality. In fact, *searching* for answers may in the end be more life-enforcing than the answers themselves.

One point must be repeated here, that Stoppard insists his plays be entertaining: "If you write a play your primary aim must be that people don't leave before the end."[9] To that should be amended Ross Wetzeon's words: "This word-wizard understands the true function of comedy is to help us define what should be taken seriously."[10]

Stoppard's language

> Language is a finite instrument crudely applied to an infinity of ideas.   *Jumpers* (51)

More than almost any living writer, Stoppard is obsessed with the many quirky irregularities of the English language. Numerous critics have observed that this interest in the curiosities of English is the result of Stoppard's immigrant status, noting that his interest is similar to other immigrant writers like Joseph Conrad and Vladimir Nabokov. The problem with this biographical perspective is that Stoppard's work is also reminiscent of many eminent native English speakers as well, notably Oscar Wilde and P. G. Wodehouse. Regardless of the reason, what is irrefutable is that Stoppard is intrigued by language, especially its simultaneous ability to illuminate and obfuscate.

Stoppard's particular talent as a stylist sometimes results in his being labeled an aesthete or formalist. Certainly his interest in Oscar Wilde and dramatic forms like farce and parody invite such labeling. In his aptly titled study *Tom Stoppard: The Artist as Critic*, Neil Sammells focuses on Stoppard's debt to celebrated aesthete Oscar Wilde and argues that Stoppard's plays are formalist, self-conscious critiques of art and the artist.[11] In a similar vein, Katherine E. Kelly argues in *Tom Stoppard and the Craft of Comedy* that Stoppard self-consciously plays with genre and medium but does so in an effort to explore the degree to which the division between art and life is "permeable."[12] By focusing on Stoppard's form and style, these critics are identifying a fundamental starting point in his search for "truth": if you are going to search for meaning, you had better be certain your tools are in working order. By way of argument and rebuttal, what Stoppard reveals is that language both is and is not up to the tasks it is generally intended to perform.

Puns, cross-talking, and dazzling but faulty rhetoric are all cause for laughter throughout Stoppard's work, but also cause for concern that language is not doing quite what it is supposed to do. Jim Hunter, in his excellent early assessment of Stoppard, makes the following observation: "The uncertainty whether to be a serious artist or a siren is one intrinsic to the nature of theatre and film. Stoppard is merely a rather remarkable example of it. This needs grasping, so as to avoid the foolishness of trying to take jokes too seriously, and equally to avoid missing the richness on offer."[13] This is the single most important point to grasp as one engages Stoppard's theatre: to be neither too analytical nor too non-analytical.

Consider the opening of *Arcadia*. Young Thomasina asks her tutor Septimus, "What is 'carnal embrace'?" to which the tutor responds, "Carnal embrace is the practice of throwing one's arms around a side of beef" (1). A laugh is virtually guaranteed at this exchange since carnal embrace does vaguely sound like it could involve a side of beef. The two are also dealing with a pathetically sterile term more apt for a lecture hall than a moonlit gazebo. Eventually, we see exactly why the play opens with this bit of laughter, for *Arcadia* will spend a good deal of energy dealing with the rich ambiguities of that thing so impotently described here as "carnal embrace." Moving from this term to other ways of describing sex, passion, and love reveals how language offers myriad options for many of our most complex thoughts and ideas, inspiring incredibly vivid precision but also frequent confusion. Curiously, both precision and confusion are often generated as much by design as by accident: consider poetry, propaganda, the unintended pun. All of these, and more, are subjects of Stoppard's scrutiny.

George Moore, Stoppard's bumblingly earnest and often accidentally witty philosopher in *Jumpers*, epitomizes the frustration of inheriting such a system of communication when he observes that "words betray the thoughts they are supposed to express. Even the most generalized truth begins to look like special pleading as soon as you trap it in language" (32–33). Here, Stoppard argues the shortcomings of language with a precision that George seems to say is impossible.

At the opening of *Professional Foul*, one character reflects on a photograph of a colleague he has just met:

> MCKENDRICK I wasn't sure it was you. Not a very good likeness.
> ANDERSON I assure you this is how I look.
> MCKENDRICK I mean your photograph . . . . The photograph is
>   younger.
> ANDERSON It must be an old photograph . . . . How odd.
> MCKENRICK Is it?
> ANDERSON Young therefore old. Old therefore young.   (44)

Older photos capture younger subjects. Here language is accurate but curiously confusing. In *Travesties*, Carr the socialite confronts Cecily the socialist:

> CECILY I am afraid that I disapprove of servants.
> CARR You are quite right to do so. Most of them are without
>   scruples.   (73)

Disapproving of a servant class is not the same as disapproving of servant behavior. The words are properly positioned, there is no desire to confuse, but confusion nevertheless occurs. Just minutes earlier Tzara is literally honest when he says to Cecily, "I haven't got a brother," to which she replies, "Don't say that! He has renounced the life of decadent nihilism" (80). Tzara's statement can be legitimately (mis)construed to mean either he has no brother or he has disowned a brother. Factuality comes face to face with its figurative twin. Then there is the conceptual running headlong into the concrete. In *The Coast of Utopia: Shipwreck*, one character boasts, "Freedom is a state of mind," to which another rejoins, "No, it's a state of not being locked up" (35).

In *Dirty Linen*, a boss asks a secretary, "You do speedwriting, I suppose?" She responds, "Yes, if given enough time" (29). Funny at first, and the secretary comes off poorly, until you realize that speedwriting does quite literally require time even if one is truly speedy, and so her comment is reasonable. The truth here undermines our presumption that all buxom secretaries (which she is) are hopelessly dumb (which she is not). Charon, the guardian of the underworld in *The Invention of Love*, announces that he is waiting to ferry a scholar and a poet across the river. The just deceased Housman says "that must be me" (2). Expecting two men – not one man of two such different professions – the ferryman is caught off guard.

There are times, too, when the words fall into place in ways that say truth has been served, but then suspicion creeps in almost immediately. Guildenstern seems to show uncharacteristically keen insight with the following burst of eloquence: "We cross our bridges when we come to them and burn them behind us, with nothing to show for our progress except a memory of the smell of smoke, and a presumption that once our eyes watered" (61). It sounds like the literal point – bridges are best burned after crossing them, and burnings result in toxic smells and unpleasant eye irritants – is designed to rise to some richly engaging, philosophically profound, metaphorical level. But it is also possible that Guildenstern is simply describing an instance of wanton destruction on this road to Elsinore. Profundity can at times be merely in the eye of the beholder.

Stoppard often moves from literal to metaphorical in ways that call attention to levels buried beneath an utterance. When Dotty cries "Help!" in *Jumpers*, her psychiatrist reassures her husband that it is nothing more than "what we psychiatrists call 'a cry for help'" (54). Then there is the precision of wit, when language adds up to more than the sum of its parts. Stoppard makes the point in the following:

> If I said to you, "The necessity of having a job is extremely inconvenient to those who like going to pubs," it would be an extremely lame remark. What it is is a very inept translation of my theoretical French edition of Oscar Wilde, the English of which is "Work is the curse of the drinking classes."[14]

Language clearly has its limitations. But it is also far better able to describe truth than conventional truth-seekers often recognize. Stoppard loves its elasticity and perpetually tests its strengths and weaknesses.

Stoppard's staged thought experiments

> Really ... your mind keeps wandering about in a senile chaos.
> *Artist Descending a Staircase* (18)

Thinking of Tom Stoppard, Kenneth Tynan recalls a passage from a letter by John Keats: "The only means of strengthening one's intellect is to make up one's mind about nothing – to let the mind be a thoroughfare for all thoughts, not a select party."[15] Openness allows for the unlikely and paves the way for new avenues of thinking. Tynan sees that as a Stoppardian strength.

In Stoppard's 1988 play *Hapgood*, we hear the story of an unproductive Soviet particle physicist who muscles his way from research into a job with Soviet state security. One night, he has a Eureka moment where his two lives – as physicist and spy – collide. Applying Heisenberg's Uncertainty Principle of trajectory and location to state security, he discovers the advantages of recruiting twins into the Soviet espionage business. This little anecdote built into *Hapgood* speaks generally to a particle-colliding process Stoppard undertakes throughout his playwriting. Stoppard likes to say that he is an aficionado of metaphysical wit, working hard to violently yoke together otherwise unconnected ideas (as Samuel Johnson once explained the term).[16] In the case of *Hapgood*, Stoppard began with a yoking-together thought experiment, wondering in what ways is a spy like a quantum of energy, in what ways are all humans like spies, and in what ways is being human like being a quantum of energy? Most of Stoppard's plays can likewise be approached as extended thought experiments. What if two minor characters in a major Shakespeare play were given centerstage? What if several intellectual titans of modernism met on neutral ground and debated their positions? How is British romanticism like chaos theory? The answers to each curious scenario lead to actions and interactions uniquely suitable for the "laboratory" of the stage.

One of Stoppard's favorite thought-experiment techniques has been to open his plays by disorienting his audience. *After Magritte* opens with a room full of characters momentarily caught in curiously contorted poses. The more sophisticated among us might pick up on the title and conclude that we are looking at a scene modeled "after," or in the style of, the Belgian surrealist artist René Magritte,[17] and we are about to enter a world of surrealistic or absurdist fantasy. But it turns out that the events of the play simply occurred following (i.e., after) a family visit to a Magritte exhibition, leaving us realizing that the title means far less than we presumed. Instead of forecasting a rather bizarre surrealistic play, the opening scene turns out to have a reasonable explanation, which suggests that the inspiration for the play may have arisen from questions like: What if there were good reasons why Magritte's paintings are so strange? Could surrealism have logical roots if we only knew more?

George Moore of *Jumpers* recounts a historically based thought experiment that Stoppard was surely pleased to have discovered:

> Meeting a friend in a corridor, Wittgenstein said: "Tell me, why do people always say it was *natural* for men to assume that the sun went around the

earth rather than that the earth was rotating?" His friend said, "Well, obviously, because it just *looks* as if the sun is going round the earth." To which the philosopher replied, "Well, what would it have looked like if it had looked as if the earth was rotating?"   (65)

Seeing a fundamental disconnect between the world and our perceptions of the world, Stoppard creates a theatre of thought experiments designed to encourage us to re-vision what is out there in ways we had not previously considered.

Change is the only constant

> The natural condition is chaos.   *Undiscovered Country* (112)

In 1973 Stoppard wrote an unproduced play/filmscript, *Galileo*. In it Stoppard gives Galileo a speech in which he ponders:

> I do not understand why perfection should be a state of rest rather than a state of change. I am very fond of this earth. It is not of course perfect, but that which I find noble and admirable in it is all to do with change. The change of a bud to a flower, of a deer feeding to a deer running, the change of a grape to wine, child to man, wood to flame; and the ash is thrown on the soil to help the buds change to flowers again. Alteration, novelty, decay, regeneration – these are not the *blemishes* of the world. Who would want a crystal globe? What use is *that* to man as created by God?[18]

The speech summarizes the outlook found in most of Stoppard's work. Perfection is a moving target, order is dynamic not static, and change is good. If Stoppard's theatre challenges the absurdist view that the world is random (and it is clear that it does challenge that view), then it also challenges the view that the world is – or should be – headed toward crystalline, static perfection. Alteration, novelty, patterns of decay and regeneration all seem to be what Stoppard seeks in his theatre.

Clearly, not everyone appreciates this vision of order, and Stoppard documents as much. In *Albert's Bridge*, a suicidal Fraser climbs a bridge span, fully intending to jump off. However, Fraser finds that from this height, "I look down at it all and find that the proportions have been re-established. My confidence is restored, by perspective" (39). The problem here is that the perspective entails withdrawal from the details of life, confirming a point Lord Malquist makes in the novel *Lord Malquist and Mr. Moon* when he epigrammatically observes, "Nothing is the history of the world viewed from a suitable distance" (8). Malquist finds order, as does Fraser (and Fraser's compatriot Albert), by withdrawing from the heady chaos of life and assuming a position of disaffected abstraction. Others find similar escapes from life's hustle and bustle in asylums, ivory towers, or jobs whose routines forcibly impose order onto life.

Then there are those who actively seek order amid life's chaos. Moon dreams of uncovering the keys to the world's order throughout *Lord Malquist and Mr. Moon*: "It occurred to him that the labyrinthine riddle of London's streets might be subjected to a single mathematical formula, one of such sophistication that it would relate the whole hopeless mess into a coherent logic" (122). The obsession of such characters to unlock the secrets of existence is far more admirable than mere escapism, but for the most part they are misguided in what exactly they are looking for. Fearing an incoherent randomness, they look beyond for a level of orderliness that simply does not exist.

So there is one group that concedes disorderliness in life, and another that doggedly insists order prevails. Then there is the third option for Stoppard, involving an ingenious middle ground vision that perceives an order that oddly enough feels like disorder given our previous disposition to see order as static and crystalline. Stoppard's hybrid philosophy – neither radical absurdist nor conventionally rationalist – finds multiple forms of expression throughout his career. Then, in 1993, finding an ally in chaos theory, he wrote *Arcadia*.

Chaotics includes cornerstone concepts that Stoppard himself had independently pursued in his art for at least two decades.[19] In his 1975 essay "Count Zero Splits the Infinite," Clive James is keenly perceptive when he sees Stoppard's *Rosencrantz and Guildenstern Are Dead* engaging the fundamentals of physics. James finds the heart of Stoppard when he recalls, "physics... ceased being Newtonian and started being modern when Einstein found himself obliged to rule out the possibility of a viewpoint at rest," all in an effort "to be precise over a greater range of events than Newtonian mechanics could accurately account for."[20] This, insists James, is Stoppard's plan, to find a way to move beyond the functional but restrictive Newtonian vision of universal order while avoiding absurdism's iconoclastic celebration of anti-rationalist meaninglessness or randomness or disorder. James was not fully aware that he was describing contemporary chaos theory, primarily because the cornerstones of the field had not yet found their way into popular consciousness. The same holds for Stoppard, unaware that other fields were viewing the world through the same glasses he was wearing. But Stoppard, much like his scientific counterparts, was pursuing answers to the question: What if the world were both orderly and disorderly at the same time?

The much-celebrated butterfly effect sums up the relatively new science of chaos theory, and in the process it can help us to understand Stoppard's theatre. The butterfly effect states that a butterfly flapping its wings in Louisiana may initiate a string of events that could lead to a massive tornado in China. Or, the same butterfly's mildly turbulent flutter could harmlessly blend into the breeze of a summer afternoon. The problem is that there is no way to predict exactly which of these options – or the myriad in-between options – will eventuate; no amount of data can predict future events with absolute certainty. Things do *cause* other things to happen, as traditional science has been reporting for centuries. But there is always the chance that something totally unexpected will arise from the exact same circumstances. What unfolds is a world that is orderly – it is governed by cause and effect – but that also has enough probabilistic wriggle room to be unpredictable in how it operates. Chaos theory teaches us that we are living in a world governed by *unpredictable determinism*: things happen in an orderly or patterned way (determinism), but – thanks to the butterfly effect – we will never be able to know with certainty how things will turn out until after they actually happen (unpredictability). And change is the new order of the day.

Speaking of *Hapgood* and *Arcadia*, his two "science" plays – which use quantum physics and chaotics, respectively – Stoppard observes:

> I thought that quantum mechanics and chaos mathematics suggested themselves as quite interesting and powerful metaphors for human behavior, not just behavior, but about the way, in the latter case, in which it suggested a determined life, a life ruled by determinism, and a life which is subject simply to random causes and effects.[21]

While he adds upon completing *Arcadia*, "I've got a funny feeling the sci [science] and phys [physics] are a phase" (84) that he will soon move beyond, the fact remains that the orderly disorderliness of chaos theory is, as James observes years earlier, what Stoppard has been doing his whole career, before, during and after *Arcadia*.

But is it art?

> Skill without imagination is craftsmanship ... Imagination without skill gives us modern art.   *Artist Descending a Staircase* (19)

Henry Carr points out in *Travesties*, "Art is absurdly overrated by artists, which is understandable, but what is strange is that it is absurdly overrated by everyone else" (46). Believing that art needs a purpose, one industrious sculptor in *Artist Descending a Staircase* solves the problem by making edible art. That of course is not a real answer. Stoppard seems most consistently to believe that art's "purpose" is to generate experiences that will make its audience reconsider and possibly even alter not *what* it thinks and feels but *the way* it thinks and feels.

Stoppard has many times famously confessed to loving theatre because it allows him to lay out multiple sides of any argument and does not force him to take sides. Uncertainty is for Stoppard an honorable state of being. One character in *Undiscovered Country* notes, "Since certainty is unattainable, entertainment value is the only justification for conversation" (130). In the face of an overwhelming uncertainty, pursuing entertainment is of course a viable option, and Stoppard does at times take that route, confessing: "When a playwright is putting lines down on paper, all he's really thinking about is that people shouldn't leave early. That's the absolute priority of plays."[22]

But there is usually something far more substantial to Stoppard's art. It is true that he is passionately committed to entertaining his guests, and it is equally true that he does not write plays to disseminate particular personal opinions about existence. In this regard he is not "political" or "moralistic" or "activist" in his art, a fact that puts him at odds with many British playwrights of his generation. But at another level he is very much a political, moralistic, and activist playwright. Consider the following:

> The *Guardian* [a London newspaper] quoted me in 14 point bold quoting Auden saying that his poems hadn't saved a single Jew from the gas chambers, and ever since then I've wanted to pay homage to Auden, or his shade, with the rider that I was making a point about the short-term and not the long-term. Briefly art – Auden or Fugard or the entire cauldron – is important because it provides the moral matrix, the moral responsibility, from which we make our judgements about the world.[23]

In the short term, "If you looked out your window and saw something . . . you felt was a cancer on society and you wanted to change it *now*, you could hardly do worse than write a play about it."[24] Art is unique in its ability to alter and strengthen the bonds that generate a "moral matrix" from which change can flow. As Stoppard asserted as far back as 1974, "our moral sensibility is laid down by art not by reportage."[25] Political activism has better venues (e.g., journalism), and agitprop theatre generally exists with an expiration date. Stoppard's theatre is designed for the contemplative long run.

Stoppard's art, in other words, works to break down general presumptions and prejudices that we all have as we strive to make sense of the world and how we should make our way through it. Lord Malquist, a somewhat unreliable source, proposes the purely aesthetic value of art by insisting that "it is the duty of an artist to leave the world decorated by some trifling and quite useless ornament" (68). But even here this sense of ornament is qualified by Malquist himself, who sees art as an ordering agent: "I find crowds extraordinarily lacking ... Taken as a whole, they have no sense of form or colour. I long to impose some aesthetic principle on them, rearrange them into art" (10). Art organizes, as it certainly does in *Travesties* where Henry Carr's shaky memories are stabilized (however unreliably) by drawing upon Oscar Wilde's *The Importance of Being Earnest*. As Carr tells the tale of his time in Switzerland during the Great War, he formulates it to conform to his recollections of Wilde's play, the result of *Earnest* having been emblazoned on Carr's consciousness early in life. This is a radical (and radically comic) way of making the case that art helps us to make sense of the world. But it is also a case Stoppard suggests we should consider.

On occasion Stoppard can present an utterly romantic vision of art, as he does with his poets and philosophers in *The Coast of Utopia*: "Every work of art is the breath of a single eternal idea breathed by God into the inner life of the artist" (*Part One: Voyage*, 39). But the problem with the ideas expressed in *The Coast of Utopia* is that they are so utopian in their almost naive idealism that it is hard to believe anything that Stoppard has his band of dreamers say. So it may be that art should be high-minded, as Stoppard's Joyce points out in *Travesties*: "An artist is the magician put among men to gratify – capriciously – their urge for immortality" (62). Or art may need to serve an opposite end, as Tzara observes, also in *Travesties*: "Now we need vandals and desecrators, simple-minded demolition men to smash centuries of baroque subtlety, to bring down the temple, and thus finally, to reconcile the shame and necessity of being an artist" (62).

Stoppard has on several occasions confessed to being inclined toward Joyce in the debate that rages in *Travesties*, observing, "Temperamentally and intellectually, I'm very much on Joyce's side." But then he also observes, "I found it persuasive to write Tzara's speech."[26] In the end, Stoppard gives neither man the winning hand. In fact we can see typical Stoppardian give-and-take in the play itself, in that it simultaneously assaults (i.e., "travesties") the apparently purposeless aestheticism of Oscar Wilde's *The Importance of Being Earnest* while at the same time paying homage by way of Stoppard's masterful integration of Wilde's play into the fabric of his own work. Among all the give and take on Stoppard's part regarding the nature of art, one thing is pretty clear: "Art deals with exceptions, not with types," as Wilde puts it in *The Invention of Love* (93). It is the only way for art to move humanity forward.

While Neil Sammells goes so far as to label Stoppard's early theatre a "Theatre of Parody," he insists that Stoppard's brand of parody is a critique (and self-critique) of the limits of whatever form it is Stoppard parodies.[27] So, for example, in *The Real Inspector Hound*, an Agatha-Christie-style thriller, Stoppard's parody tests the limits of the murder mystery conventions that underpin the genre. Stoppard seems to particularly like the mystery form, returning to it throughout his career in often thinly disguised ways, from *Jumpers* to *Hapgood*, *Indian Ink* and beyond, testing the limits of conventional investigational skills – playing with cause and effect – throughout his theatre. When Stoppard explores causality in his fundamentally realistic format – as in *A Walk on the Water*, *Night and Day*, and *The Real Thing* – the very conventions of realistic exposition are scrutinized, with frequently unsettling results. The opening scene of *The Real Thing*, for example, draws us into a world of betrayal that turns out to be pure illusion (it is a play within the play). Then, as the play unfolds, the opening scene turns out to be a largely true depiction of betrayal and loss, leaving us to wonder whether we were seeing "the real thing" in act one even though it was not really the real thing. Stoppard loves to set up expectations based on conventional practices and then demonstrate how these expectations hinder and even thwart us on our paths to understanding. Recall how the title *After Magritte* lures us into unfounded presumptions. For Stoppard, artistic conventions and expectations become the argument that he rebuts in an effort to awaken audiences to more flexible thinking.

All of this takes talent, of course. In a postmodern world where high and low "art" freely commingle, and where "art" as a term is regularly called into existential/ontological doubt, Stoppard comfortably stands out as a throwback to a more traditional vision: "An artist is someone who is gifted in some way which enables him to do something more or less well which can only be done badly or not at all by someone not thus gifted." The passage curiously exists in both *Artist Descending a Staircase* (19) and *Travesties* (38), suggesting that Stoppard particularly likes the point. It is much more epigrammatically stated in his famous "Skill without imagination is craftsmanship and gives us many useful objects such as wickerwork picnic baskets. Imagination without skill gives us modern art" (*Artist Descending a Staircase*, 19). And it is the central position held by Henry, the playwright (and perhaps Stoppard's alter ego) in *The Real Thing*. Henry argues that his art requires something more than gritty determination. He famously uses a cricket-bat metaphor, noting that the bat looks like a mere cudgel but is in fact "several pieces of particular wood cunningly put together in a certain way so that ... if you get it right, the cricket ball will travel two hundred yards in four seconds" (51). What an artist/playwright is "trying to do is to write cricket bats, so that when you throw up an idea and give it a little knock it might . . . *travel*" (51). Plays, for Henry – and possibly for Stoppard too – are put together like cricket bats, cunningly constructed things of beauty given the added function of making ideas *travel*. This point taps into something Stoppard often repeated early in his career: "What I try to do, is to end up contriving the perfect marriage between the play of ideas and farce, or perhaps even high comedy."[28] Though he moves beyond the farce and high comedy of his early days, what is crucial to emphasize is that Stoppard's plays throughout his career are constructed to send forth ideas in the most cunning of ways.

So the best of his plays are more than entertainment designed simply to generate laughter. Stoppard may see journalism and politics as game changers in the short term, but clearly he sees theatre as its own sort of game changer. Journalism and politics cudgel for immediate effect while art sends ideas flying deep into our consciousnesses with a little knock. As a result, "art doesn't have to be true like a theorem" (*Coast of Utopia, Part One: Voyage*, 16) in ways that political treatises must, because art expresses truth beyond reasoned explica-tion and through means other than logic. *The Coast of Utopia* also reminds us that a "poem can't be written by an act of will. When the rest of us are trying our hardest to be present, a real poet goes absent" (*Part One: Voyage*, 38). Journalism takes sweat and practice as does art. But art also involves something that cannot be taught or passed on in the same way a skill can be taught. The result is something that can uniquely "cheat oblivion, because only the artist can say, 'Look on my works, ye mighty, and despair'" (*Indian Ink*, 44; the quotation is from Shelley's "Ozymandias").

On human nature and human consciousness

> Consciousness is where it's at.   *Rock'n'Roll* (47)

Stoppard's plays challenge the generally accepted perspective that what humans do is passively observe a ready-made world passing before our senses, a challenge that in turn questions the idea that "I" am somehow separate from (and superior to) the rest of the world. Instead of consciousness being a *tabula rasa* (blank slate) absorbing reality through the senses in a disengaged, objec-tive manner, Stoppard insists that our minds actively interact with the infor-mation they receive from the "outside" world, actively contributing to the make-up of what we think of as "reality."

It is not a big section in *Rock'n'Roll*, but it is an important one. Max, the last dedicated Communist in the Western world, is also known for his two academic

books, *Class and Consciousness* and *Masses and Materialism* (43), which identify
him as a specialist in materialist consciousness theory. Max is determined to
follow the Marxist agenda of liberating "reason from our ancestral bog of myth
and claptrap" (46), and he proceeds by arguing that the brain is nothing more
than "a biological machine for thinking. If it wasn't for the merely technical
problem of understanding how it works, we could make one out of – beer cans"
(47). Max even argues that mysterious things that emanate from the brain, like
"inspiration," are actually "so many neuron-firings whizzing about the cortex"
(46), and he admits to liking the image of the brain as a pinball machine. This is,
of course, a radically materialist interpretation of the brain. It is also a point of
view that has real merit according to some theorists in the scientific community
who argue that some day we will be able to create thinking machines – and even
feeling machines – every bit as complex as human beings. After all, according to
this point of view, everything ultimately boils down to chemical and neural
responses to our environment. Even in *Travesties*, Stoppard's masterful play
about false memory, befuddled Carr uses a fairly common mechanistic metaphor to explain his confusion: "Incidentally, you may or may not have noticed
that I got my wires crossed a bit here and there" (64).

On the other hand, Max's intellectual sparring partner Lenka goes back into
the distant evolutionary past and argues that as humans developed into the
thinking machines we have become, "we lost something older than reason, and
stronger than your pinball machine which thinks it's in love" (46). Lenka's point
of view is one we see pop up throughout Stoppard's theatre where reason and
logic – those pinball devices of the thinking machine – reveal their limits as
powerful and vexing feelings short-circuit the machine. Stoppard reminds us that
there likely is something more to consciousness than mere neural connectivity.

In turn, the problem with challenging the thinking machine idea is that it
very nearly forces us to conclude that consciousness derives from some
mysterious, immortal breath of god. In fact this is an argument that George
Moore tries to prove in *Jumpers*, though all he finally proves is what most
of us already know, namely that the existence of god is a rationally unprovable proposition that boils down to faith. Moore explains his point in a
bumbling-seeming but surprisingly insightful way: "I don't claim to *know*
that God exists, I only claim that he does without my knowing it, and while
I claim as much I do not claim to know as much; indeed I cannot know and
God knows I cannot" (60). Can we "know" even when the logical/rational
devices of the brain cannot confirm what we know? For Stoppard, this is
where life gets interesting.

So we have a play like *Travesties* where Carr takes the sort of cognitive leaps
that a mechanistic vision of consciousness would simply consider a systemic

malfunction. But Carr's malfunctions reach for a reality that exists beyond what mere passive fact-gathering machines can grasp, revealing the point that truth is far more than a collection of facts. For his television play *Squaring the Circle, Poland 1980–81*, Stoppard coined the term "faction" – a blend of fact and fiction – and has a narrator actually announce about this "documentary" that "Everything is true except the words and the pictures" (191–92). And then there is the "factional" *Shakespeare in Love*, an imaginative invention that some would argue captures the "real" Will Shakespeare better than any journalist, historian, or biographer has yet done.

Stoppard's imaginative process leads him to challenge the rationalist conclusion that humans are complex word processors. But his intellectual curiosity also leaves him uncomfortable with believing that imagination and creativity are the gifts of the gods.

In *Hapgood*, Stoppard suggests that consciousness may in fact be a bit like the structure of the atom, but not the atom we learned about in grade school. Making sense of the contemporary vision of the atom, the quantum physicist in the play, Kerner, notes that if an atom had a fist-sized nucleus, its electrons would flit about like moths in a cathedral, occasionally colliding in their jerky and unpredictable trajectories, and generating new matter as they go. Particles do not behave in orderly, mechanistic ways (staying within certain orbits, etc.) but pursue *chaotic* paths that have an orderliness reminiscent of the butterfly effect, making unpredictable but determined "quantum leaps" as they go. And so it goes that *Hapgood* suggests that ideas in the brain flit like moths in a cathedral and also collide in jerky and unpredictable trajectories, generating new ideas/thoughts at the most unlikely of moments.[29] Basically, Stoppard is working to make sense of his mind's surprising facility by giving it credit for a creativity that undermines mechanism while also avoiding the need to turn to a "breath of god" interpretation. In its way, this theoretical model *is* mechanistic but not ploddingly linear, rational but not predictable.

Stoppard also uses quantum mechanics to suggest that human beings comprise split or multiple personalities/consciousnesses. Speaking about *Hapgood*, he suggests: "The dual nature of light works for people as well as things, and the one you meet in public is simply the working majority of that person."[30] It is interesting to note the number of times throughout his career that Stoppard uses doubles and split personalities. Stoppard himself observes "I could write an awfully good book about The Plays of Tom Stoppard – to me, it's so obvious: many of my plays are about unidentical twins, about double acts."[31] It is important to note that Stoppard does not suggest humans are inherently schizophrenic so much as that even the most normal of individuals experience issues of cohabitation. He even offers a logic that gives coherence to this multiplicity. In *Professional Foul*, catastrophe theory is introduced, along with a geometry that actually allows parallel lines to intersect. One character observes:

> The two lines are on the same plane. (*He holds out his flat hand, palm down, above the scored lines.*) They're the edges of the same plane – it's in three dimensions, you see – and if you twist the plane in a certain way, into what we call a catastrophe curve, you get a model of the sort of behaviour we find in the real world. There's a point – the catastrophe point – where your progress along one line of behaviour jumps you into the opposite line; the principle reverses itself at the point where a rational man would abandon it.   (168–69)

At a critical or "catastrophe" point along a scale of human thought, an almost irrational shift in thought occurs. For example, "thou shalt not kill" is a standard refrain we all almost unthinkingly accept. But here mathematics rationally illustrates that "wrong" behavior can at times become right behavior, that at certain points along the curve killing *is* justified. "Thou shalt not kill" is tested in *Hapgood*, "thou shalt not lie or steal" is tested in *Professional Foul*, "thou shalt not covet" is tested in *The Real Thing*. Each reveals catastrophe point reversals of one sort or another, unearthing split personalities among normal humans throughout. And so believing contradictory points and behaving in contradictory ways may not be as illogical as standardly assumed. Perhaps there is a method to the madness of human inconsistency and an explanation for the apparent existence of multiple selves cohabiting a single skin.

Everywhere in Stoppard's work, there are instances where the mechanistic, linear worldview is confronted and undermined. Consciousness is at the heart of Stoppard's assault on a too rigid vision of the universe. It interacts with reality to generate truths that extend human sight, knowledge, and selfhood beyond the grasp of the merely rational and linear. The world leaps up to meet us, but we also leap up to meet it.

The political animal

> Theories don't guarantee social justice, social justice tells you if a theory is any good.   *Squaring the Circle* (251)

Stoppard has said on numerous occasions that his plays "must be entirely untouched by any suspicion of usefulness" and that he "should have the courage of my lack of conviction,"[32] suggesting that social change is the farthest thing from Stoppard's playwriting mind. This position stands out for a man whose career spans a period in Western theatre history that has been largely left-leaning and very politically active. As a result Stoppard has frequently been criticized for a lack of political engagement and also for not leaning far enough to the left when he does become engaged. But he is not alone among theatre practitioners in this regard. Kenneth Tynan, for one, sees Stoppard as part of a group of "cool, apolitical stylists, like Harold Pinter, the late Joe Orton, Christopher Hampton (*The Philanthropist*), Alan Ayckbourn (*The Norman Conquests*), Simon Gray (*Otherwise Engaged*)."[33]

On a purely personal level, Stoppard concedes, "I always thought of myself as a conservative not in a sort of ideological way ... [because] what I like and don't like certainly doesn't divide up into things that the Conservative Party or Labour Party does."[34] In a 2008 interview, Stoppard the lower-case conservative labeled himself a "timid libertarian."[35] Kenneth Tynan summarized Stoppard's conservatism as one that believes in "the intrinsic merit of individualism, ... a universe in which everything is relative yet in which moral absolutes exist," and "the probability that this paradox can be resolved only if we accept the postulate of a presiding morality," concluding that Stoppard believes "the difference between good and evil is obvious to any reasonable person."[36] In sum, Stoppard reports that striving for "human solidarity was a better bet than class solidarity."[37] He has taken a number of activist stances against totalitarian government abuses, but particular homeland political issues rarely find their way into Stoppard's theatre: "I don't lose any sleep if a policeman in Durham beats somebody up, because I know it's an exceptional case ... What worries me is not the bourgeois exception but the totalitarian norm."[38]

Stoppard, as quoted above, repeatedly insists that if your goal is direct and immediate change of a certain situation, "you could hardly do worse than write a play about it." In this same interview, he tells a story about a news reporter who "wrote a story on wages paid by British companies in South Africa ... [W]ithin 48 hours the wages have gone up. I can't do that. I'll never be able to do that. Athol Fugard will never be able to do that, not by writing plays." But Stoppard firmly believes that "it's because of people like Athol Fugard that the editor of the *Guardian* realised that the reporter's piece was worth leading the paper with. To stretch a point: our moral sensibility is laid down by art not by reportage." He then concludes: "It is said that Alexander II freed the serfs in 1861 partly after reading Turgenev's *Sportsman's Sketches*, short pieces about Russian peasantry. Probably what happened was that the time was right for the book and for freeing the serfs."[39]

These observations come from a 1974 interview, but Stoppard's views appear to have changed very little. If the goal is to effect immediate change, try journalism or politics. If the goal is a long-term one of effecting foundational changes in perspective or consciousness, then art/theatre is the better option. Stoppard repeats the point that "Public postures have the configuration of private derangement"[40] on numerous occasions both in plays and during interviews. The point is that in order to change public policy, there is first a need to alter personal sentiment. Stoppard says, for example, that *Jumpers* is not "a play about politics, nor is it a play about ideology," adding: "On the other hand the play reflects my belief that all political acts have a moral basis to them and are meaningless without it."[41]

When interested in politics, Stoppard has been willing to use his celebrity to militate against human rights violations in general, such as when in December 1976 he spoke at a rally in London's Trafalgar Square against Soviet abuse, or when in 1977 he visited Moscow and Leningrad as part of Amnesty International's "Prisoner of Conscience" campaign for justice. He also worked during this time with Czech playwright, political dissident, and future president Václav Havel. Out of that period came several important stage and television scripts, including *Squaring the Circle, Poland 1980–81, Cahoot's Macbeth, Professional Foul,* and *Every Good Boy Deserves Favor.* And there are his later works as well: Stoppard's *Coast of Utopia* highlights nineteenth-century Europe's spirit of revolution while *Rock'n'Roll* reflects upon the Czech Republic's Velvet Revolution of 1989. What each piece has in common is a focus on the breakdown of social order stemming from violations of individual rights that occurred as a result of restrictions on free speech. For Stoppard, restricting free speech is the source of virtually all injustice, a point that surfaces most directly but far from exclusively in *Night and Day,* his play about journalists.

Stoppard's ostensible conservatism does include "liberal" support for collective rights but only insofar as they grow out of individual rights. In the case of totalitarianism, the individual disappears under the authority of the group, and that is clearly not a good thing for Stoppard. But disregarding larger human dynamics can be problematic as well. A play like *Indian Ink* turns "political" when it becomes apparent that colonial British freedoms come at the expense of native Indian rights. And in *Jumpers,* Stoppard debates under what circumstances people will give up their freedoms for others, wondering if altruism is really a human possibilty.[42]

In *The Dog It Was That Died, Neutral Ground,* and *Hapgood,* Stoppard focuses on characters in the politically ambiguous position of being double or triple agents, revealing that it is immaterial which ideological side you're on if each side sacrifices the rights of the individual in the name of dogma. In *The Dog It Was That Died,* Blair tries to remind Purvis why he should remain with the West. But Purvis stabs at Western vulnerabilities when he asks what freedom is if it "merely benefits the people who already have the edge?" (18).

In *The Coast of Utopia, Part Three: Salvage*, the point resurfaces: historically speaking, one character reminds us, "poverty and liberty go together" (78). Tyranny and totalitarianism do pose serious problems for individual rights, but their ideological opposites are not without blemish.

Stoppard is impatient with idealists flitting on the edge of action. As the character Herzen in *The Coast of Utopia* says to Karl Marx, "A distant end is not an end but a trap. The end we work for must be closer, a labourer's wage, the pleasure in the work done, the summer lightning of personal happiness" (*Part Three: Salvage*, 119). George Moore in *Jumpers* can earnestly debate the virtues of ethical absolutes and altruism, but he loses our sympathies when he cannot see clearly enough to help his own wife. Idealists throughout *The Coast of Utopia* plot paths to the distant shore of social justice, but their abstract enthusiasms lead at best to inaction and at worst to actual death and destruction. In the defense of an idea, people starve and die.

Perhaps longing just a bit for the engaged and activist days of the 1960s and his own active anti-Communist days of the late 1970s and 1980s, Stoppard allows one of his *Rock'n'Roll* characters to bemoan the fact that Britain (and Western democracies in general) have lost their activist edge: "This place has lost its nerve ... It's a democracy of obedience. They're frightened to use their minds in case their minds tell them heresy. They apologise for history. They apologise for good manners. They apologise for difference" (102–03). As we move solidly into the twenty-first century, Stoppard is clearly looking for a more aggressive collective intellect even as he maintains respect for individual freedoms. But his theatre will not be the primary instrument of such change.

To sum up

> I forget the third thing.   *Travesties* (99)

Somewhere along a continuum of argument and rebuttal that includes action/inaction, reason/faith, art/craft, art/politics, creativity/linearity, randomness/order, and illusion/reality lies the real Tom Stoppard. But as we learn from physics, like a quantum trick of light, Stoppard relishes the idea that "A lot can be said about my work [that] is true without its opposite necessarily being false."[43]

As noted earlier, Stoppard frequently says he likes the idea that his plays exhibit the kind of wit that the eighteenth century described as violently yoking together two ideas in order to create something new. New combinations and recombinations make for a dynamics that reaches to the core of Stoppard's universe: change is good.

Chapter 3

The breakthrough years

> We drift down time, clutching at straws. But what good's a brick to
> a drowning man?   *Rosencrantz and Guildenstern Are Dead* (108)

What some critics describe as Stoppard's "overnight success" with *Rosencrantz and Guildenstern Are Dead* was actually anything but overnight given that Stoppard had been a professional writer for nearly a decade. Overnight or not, Stoppard certainly welcomed the recognition. His other major accomplishment during the period, the novel *Lord Malquist and Mr. Moon*, was not such a critical or popular sensation. It is, however, a work that stands the test of time and still awaits the full attention it deserves.

Two early works

> There's two of everyone ... I mean if he's the same in the pub as he is
> with us, then he's had it.   *Enter a Free Man* (10)

Stoppard's career prior to his breakthrough *Rosencrantz and Guildenstern Are Dead* is primarily that of an apprentice learning his craft by imitation. *A Walk on the Water* (written 1960, rewritten and produced for television 1963), later retitled *Enter a Free Man* (1968), is his first full-length play. In interviews Stoppard playfully retitles it *Flowering Death of a Salesman*, combining Robert Bolt's *Flowering Cherry* (1957) and Arthur Miller's *Death of a Salesman* (1949),[1] which – like Stoppard's play – are about aging men who lose touch with reality. Stoppard acknowledges that first plays such as his "tend to be the sum of all the plays you have seen of a type you can emulate technically and have admired."[2]

To that end he calls his other significant work from this early period, *The Gamblers* (written 1961–62, produced 1965), "*Waiting for Godot in the Condemned Cell.*"[3]

Enter a Free Man centers on George Riley, a wistful dreamer carrying on as an inventor waiting to strike it rich while his wife and daughter support him and his quixotic fantasies. His curiously impractical inventions include a pipe that stays lit only if smoked upside-down, a bottle opener for which no bottle cap currently exists, an indoor plant watering system that tends to flood, and a reusable letter envelope whose glitches are not quite worked out as the play opens. *Enter a Free Man* has most of the trappings of a play following the kitchen sink tradition of John Osborne, the British playwright who in 1956 made lower-middle-class blue-collar theatre popular with his famous angry young man, Jimmy Porter, the protagonist in *Look Back in Anger*. Other playwrights followed suit, generating a politically charged theatre that rivaled the left-leaning American theatre of Arthur Miller and Tennessee Williams.

But as Stoppard's full career amply illustrates, gritty realistic portrayals of working-class Britain is not a particular Stoppardian strength. What is interesting about *Enter a Free Man* is how Stoppard manipulates this much-imitated kitchen sink realism to his own interests. Curiously, critics on occasion have read these breaks with convention as being more intellectually consequential than they really are. For example, there are times when realistic character consistency is sacrificed for what Victor L. Cahn identifies as "classic example[s] of absurdist dialogue, much like passages in the plays of Beckett, Ionesco, and Pinter."[4] Cahn offers an example:

> HARRY All Japanese inventors are small.
> CARMEN They're small people.
> HARRY Very small. Short.
> RILEY The little man.
> HARRY The little people!
> RILEY Look at the transistor!
> HARRY Very small!
> RILEY Japanese!
> CARMEN Gurkhas are short.
> HARRY But exceedingly brave for their size.
> CARMEN Fearless.
> RILEY (*furiously*) What are you talking about?   (15)

While the running gag here may appear "absurdist," it is more likely that such exchanges like this have music hall roots and are merely inserted to get a laugh.

And laughter for Stoppard is more important than either realist consistency or absurdist consequence.

Elsewhere, Riley quotes Rousseau's "A man is born free and everywhere he is in chains" (13), making a point that is clearly central to the play. But the point is made by violating the convention of character consistency, given that Riley is not an educated man and is very unlikely to be familiar with Rousseau. Stoppard, however, reveals even at this early stage that he is less interested in rules of characterization than in a pithy turn of phrase. This dialogic break with realist convention will eventually become a Stoppard hallmark, a point he plainly concedes when he notes in 1974 that "all my people speak the same way, with the same cadences and sentence structures. They speak as I do."[5] This is, of course, perfectly acceptable theatrical practice, but it does not fall into the particular tradition of kitchen sink realism.

The matter of realist consistency aside, George Riley is an interesting study. He is a man Stoppard will reintroduce in several guises in the coming years, a character who is, as Susan Rusinko notes, "a simplified antecedent of the complex Rosencrantz and Guildenstern, Moon, George Moore, Joyce, Lenin, and others in later works who insist on questioning things or escaping from the chains that bind."[6] Tynan sees Riley as the first of Stoppard's characters "who have nothing to pit against the hostility of society and the indifference of the chaos except their obstinate conviction that individualism is sacrosanct."[7]

To achieve that end in this play, Stoppard utilizes setting in ways his realist peers and predecessors do not, exploiting a split stage (showing the home and the pub) to highlight what will become another of Stoppard's major interests: the multiplicity of personalities inhering in each individual. Aging, absent-minded, unemployable, George Riley lives in two worlds, and those two worlds reveal richly contradictory dimensions. Using concurrent rather than sequential settings highlights the point. We see a world of self-delusion as it takes several forms, reminding Katherine E. Kelly that the entire family "develops 'life lies' as elaborate and essential as those propping up the Werle family in Ibsen's *The Wild Duck* and the drunkards in O'Neill's *The Iceman Cometh*."[8] The real world is a dull, life-sapping place, and survival requires illusion, no matter how flimsy and transparent it may be. Stoppard's themes may be derivative in this instance, but his use of the stage shows signs of something different on the horizon.

The Gamblers is a Beckettian dialogue between a condemned Prisoner and his Jailer, who in the end switch roles. The play opens shortly after a revolution is put down. The politically indifferent Prisoner had joined the uprising only because he believed the coup would succeed while the Jailer, a supporter of the revolution's ideals, held back his support because he feared it would fail.

Taking advantage of the Jailer's romantic notions about revolution, the Prisoner manipulates the less savvy Jailer and convinces him to take responsibility for his beliefs. As a result, the pragmatic Prisoner survives while the idealistic Jailer is convinced to head to the gallows shouting slogans lauding the revolution. John Fleming notes that the theme anticipates Stoppard's later work: "Though the conflict is ideological and political," success and failure "are based on pragmatics, not convictions," adding, "As in other Stoppard works, recurring themes are the relativity of perspectives and the importance of context to determine meaning."[9] In an observation obliquely relating to *The Gambler*, Stoppard's friend Derek Marlowe once observed of Stoppard, "I don't think that there's anything he would go to the guillotine for."[10] Though the ideas here are interesting and do anticipate Stoppard's pragmatic stand on political matters, the play is not a strong one, and Stoppard has forbidden future production.

Rosencrantz and Guildenstern Are Dead: living and dying in theatre time

> Half of what he said meant something else, and the other half didn't mean anything at all.   *Rosencrantz and Guildenstern Are Dead* (57)

Rosencrantz and Guildenstern Are Dead went through numerous drafts before finding its way onto the stage more or less in its current form. Changes include moving from verse to prose and shifting most of the play from England (where the heroes meet King Lear) to Elsinore Castle (Hamlet's home turf). A version was optioned in 1965 by the Royal Shakespeare Company, but the RSC let the option lapse. In the summer of 1966 the amateur Oxford Theatre Group asked Stoppard's agent Kenneth Ewing for permission to mount the play at the Edinburgh Fringe Festival. Ewing agreed, and the play received a generally lukewarm reception until Ronald Bryden of London's *Observer* weighed in with, "It's the most brilliant debut by a young playwright since John Arden's."[11] Kenneth Tynan, a literary agent working for Laurence Olivier at the National Theatre, reports, "Minutes after reading Bryden's piece, I cabled Stoppard, requesting a script. Olivier liked it as much as I did, and within a week we had bought it."[12] Finding a place in the theatre's season and reworking the script to accommodate the professional opinions of the National Theatre directors was a hectic business, but the play opened in April 1967 to rave reviews and instant fame for the young playwright.

   Rosencrantz and Guildenstern Are Dead takes the opportunity to ask what two minor characters in a play of great consequence may be thinking as the events swirling about them overwhelm their existences and send them off to their doom. In addition to comparisons to Beckett and Pirandello, Kenneth Tynan suggests that the play is influenced by Kafka's "enigmatic fables." He reminds us also that Oscar Wilde wrote about these two minor characters in *De Profundis* with the sort of fascination we can presume Stoppard also felt.[13] And T. S. Eliot's influence, by way of "The Love Song of J. Alfred Prufrock," is virtually self-evident:

> No! I am not Prince Hamlet, nor was meant to be;
> Am an attendant lord, one that will do
> To swell a progress, start a scene or two.

Several people have also noted that W. S. Gilbert (of Gilbert and Sullivan fame) wrote an 1891 farce called *Rosencrantz and Guildenstern*. But for all the inter-textual connections people have made, Stoppard insists (while reflecting in 1974 upon the play), "The chief interest and objective was to exploit a situation which seemed to me to have enormous dramatic and comic potential," adding, "What was actually calculated was to entertain a roomful of people with the situation of Rosencrantz and Guildenstern at Elsinore."

Stoppard's goals may have been simple at a conscious level, but Stoppard does admit that "one is the victim and beneficiary of one's subconscious all the time," confessing also (though slightly less convincingly), "I must say I didn't know what the word 'existential' meant until it was applied to *Rosencrantz*." Later in the same interview he observes, "With *Rosencrantz*, whatever lessons could be drawn from it, they were all just implied and not necessarily by me at that."[14] Among the play's detractors, Robert Brustein was the most outspoken, observing that the play "is a theatrical parasite, feeding off *Hamlet*, *Waiting for Godot*, and *Six Characters in Search of an Author* – Shakespeare provides the characters, Pirandello the technique, and Beckett the tone with which the Stoppard play proceeds."[15] Curiously, even if Brustein's summary were accurate and complete, he seems inadvertently to be praising Stoppard with faint damnation, describing as he does a pretty admirable accomplishment of theatrical dexterity. Add to this point the fact that Brustein's summary is actually incomplete at best, given that the play is laden with Stoppardian originality. For one, Stoppard's "Shakespearean" characters are men whose curiosity, flaws, qualities of endearment, and even cowardice are Stoppard's own inventions nowhere to be found in the original work. Stoppard starts with sources but ends with a work that is anything but derivative.

The play opens with "Two Elizabethans passing the time in a place without any visible character" (11).[16] Are we in Elizabethan England, medieval Denmark, or contemporary Britain – or are we simply "in the theatre"? There are no clear indicators, though there is plenty of evidence throughout the play that Stoppard never quite wants us to forget we are in the theatre ("Give us this day our daily cue," 102). Or since the title says the characters are dead, maybe this is hell. Stoppard's intentionally ambiguous posture allows any number of readings and production decisions.

By far the most memorable bit about the play's beginning is the opening's now famous coin-toss episode. One character is tossing what will be over one hundred heads-up coins, betting on tails and losing every toss to his friend in this incredibly improbable string of bad luck. The other character is more embarrassed for his friend than he is amazed at the near impossibility of what he is witnessing. Guildenstern (we find out) is more thoughtfully interested in the cosmic implications and not concerned at all by this spectacularly unfortunate "redistribution of wealth" (16). He comes up with a list of why this improbability is happening, which includes: he is willing it as an atonement for some unremembered past transgression; time has stopped; it is the result of divine intervention; it is merely radical evidence that each coin toss is indeed as likely to come up heads as tails. Then he proceeds to a couple of twisted syllogisms. But none of Guildenstern's reasoning leads to an adequate answer. This kind of logical dead end dominates almost every aspect of the play. It always feels like they are on the right path to an answer, but they never quite get to it.

It is primarily because reason and logic fail Rosencrantz and Guildenstern at every turn that many critics see the play as endorsing an absurdist vision of universal meaninglessness, paying homage to Beckett and his hapless tramps in *Waiting for Godot*.[17] But Felicia Londré is correct to note, "Despite such affinities with the Theatre of the Absurd, Stoppard is not an absurdist at heart. The metaphysical anguish ... is really only a literary/philosophical exercise, not a profound vision of the universe."[18] Stoppard concedes that we are stuck in the middle of a world that is hard to understand. It might even be that we will never understand the really important things in life, but that does not mean the universe is meaningless. And – here is a true Stoppardian question – is our inability to uncover life's persistent questions really a bad thing? The questions can overwhelm us at times, but we should not allow them to afflict us with Prufrockian paralysis.

In *Rosencrantz and Guildenstern Are Dead* – and elsewhere – Stoppard puts forward numerous ideas with certain degrees of conviction and then submits alternatives which in themselves contain comparable degrees of validity. What is left is the suggestion that the process of argument and rebuttal is itself a way of living life amid uncertainty. The play's famous verbal tennis match is visual evidence of this point, wherein the two men literally make a game out of asking questions, complete with penalties for responding to questions with answers.

Guildenstern is the one who tries to understand why the two men are where they are, what they are supposed to be doing, and how what's going on around them actually happens. Exasperated and near the end of all patience, toward the end of the play he blurts out: "All we get is incidents! Dear God, is it too much to expect a little sustained action?" (118). Speaking in clearly theatrical terms, what he wants is a string of actions that he can use to explain where he has been and where he is going. For him that is what meaning is all about: "Each move is dictated by the previous one – that is the meaning of order" (60). In a nutshell, Guildenstern – and Rosencrantz, too – subscribes to the idea of a rational, causal, orderly universe, or at least he is trying to.

In his film version of the play (completed over twenty years after the play was first produced), Stoppard inserts a string of visual gags that goes a long way to helping us understand Guildenstern and his pursuit of truth. What we see, in passing, is Rosencrantz picking up a shuttlecock and Indian club. He thinks for a second and then watches them as he drops them to the floor, noticing that they fall at the same rate of speed. This is one of Galileo's famous refutations of Aristotle, who thought heavier objects fell faster than lighter ones. But when he shows Guildenstern, Rosencrantz uses a croquet ball and a feather. The feather acts like feathers do, and Rosencrantz's discovery falls on skeptical eyes. Next, an apple falls on Rosencrantz's head, sparking what must be a Newtonian thought, but Rosencrantz is interrupted and moves on. Then Rosencrantz notices four clay pots hanging together on a clothes line, each touching the other. When he nudges an end pot, the opposite-end pot reacts. He has discovered energy transference through this "Newton's cradle." But when he shows Guildenstern, Rosencrantz nudges things too hard, and the clay pots shatter on contact. The same near miss occurs when Rosencrantz harnesses steam power to stir a pot. And when he takes a bath, he discovers the Archimedian principle of displacement as he rises and settles into his tub. But nothing comes of any of these observations. These are the kind of discoveries that have been held up as great human breakthroughs, but Stoppard's point seems to be that even when they *are* discovered, they really get us nowhere when it comes to matters of true import, like fate, destiny, and free will.

For important matters, the Player is the lynchpin in this play. When Rosencrantz and Guildenstern bemoan their situation, the Player is the one who says, "Uncertainty is the normal state" (66). The Player thrives under that singular assumption while Rosencrantz and Guildenstern are bound to the old ways, searching for certainty as an all-or-nothing proposition. The Player explains himself by saying first, "There's a design at work in all art – surely you know that? Events must play themselves out to aesthetic, moral, and logical conclusion" (79). He has aptly adapted Hamlet's musings on destiny (the biblically sourced

"There's a divinity that shapes our ends" and "There is special providence in the fall of a sparrow") to his own peculiar end. But whereas Hamlet sees fate controlling all existence, the Player only goes so far as to concede that there is a divinity that shapes our stage, adding the telling point that "Between 'just desserts' and 'tragic irony' we are given quite a lot of scope for our particular talent" (79). The Player insists that there is freedom to stretch and move with lively relish even as we progress to an inexorable end. Unpredictable determinism surfaces even at this early stage in Stoppard's career.

Stoppard literally places this idea right under the feet of his hapless heroes when he takes them on the sea journey to England. Guildenstern, the pensive one, says about boats, "We can move, of course, change direction, rattle about, but our movement is contained within a larger one that carries us along as inexorably as the wind and current" (122). Through this model, one could argue that there is a destiny within which we have options: we are headed to a final destination, but as we move toward that end we have an almost infinite number of *free* decisions to make. John Fleming observes, "The image is one of free will, but within constraints – of limited freedom within a larger, determined course."[19]

Within this world of uncertainty, the Player thrives on that consummate actor's philosophy, that we are nothing if our actions are not witnessed by other human beings. The Player declares, "We pledged our identities, secure in the conventions of our trade, that someone would be watching. And, then, gradually, no one was. We were caught high and dry ... The silence was unbreakable, it imposed itself upon us; it was obscene" (64). To be is to be perceived, or so goes the claim by eighteenth-century Irish philosopher George Berkeley – and the Player. The Player believes that nothing is worse than losing connection to others. At very least the consolation that Rosencrantz and Guildenstern share is that they go through life with each other as audience.

Both men, however, seem to under-appreciate companionship and obsess over more abstract matters like free will and destiny. Tying themselves up in knots, they frequently think to do something and then rethink it when they think that that was maybe what they were fated to think to do:

> ROS I could jump over the side. That would put a spoke in their wheel.
> GUIL Unless they're counting on it.
> ROS I'll remain on board. That'll put a spoke in their wheel.   (108)

How will they ever know that they are exercising free will?

In the end, Rosencrantz and Guildenstern occupy their time poorly by pursuing questions they cannot answer and paralytically avoiding actions that could have been significant. They do nothing to help their "friend" Hamlet when they discover that they carry a letter ordering his execution, and they do nothing when they read the letter that Hamlet has swapped. They read their own death warrants and go to the gallows befuddled but without resistance. Is it fate?

For those who insist on answers, *Rosencrantz and Guildenstern Are Dead* offers little satisfaction, though particular productions may choose to draw from the play's many suggestive possibilities, treating it with the same multiplicity of approaches with which *Hamlet* itself is often treated. For example, a 1992 Tel Aviv (Israel) production of *Rosencrantz and Guildenstern Are Dead* was reported to capture the heart of state tyranny by creating a world of collective terror where everyone is a spy by force and where everyone in the end loses.[20] Stoppard's own film version can also be viewed as drawing on the play's potential as a commentary on political terror and collateral damage.

Whatever the particular interpretation, however, the play reveals generally that most of us can do little more than claim to be temporary travellers making our ways through a cold and hostile environment. *Rosencrantz and Guildenstern Are Dead* suggests that as we make our way, we should look for smooth sailing, play the game with gusto, burn our bridges after we cross them, strike while the iron is hot, and play our parts to the fullest even to our last breaths. In a play that playfully presents and then mixes its myriad metaphors, Stoppard agrees it "can be interpreted in existential terms, as well as in other terms." He adds, though, that "the element which I find most valuable is the one that other people are put off by – that is, that there is very often *no* single, clear statement in my plays."[21]

Lord Malquist and Mr. Moon: a novel idea

> Since we cannot hope for order let us withdraw with style from the chaos.   *Lord Malquist and Mr. Moon* (21)

Published in 1966, Stoppard's one and only novel, *Lord Malquist and Mr. Moon*, did not receive much attention when it was released, and though it has been reprinted several times, it still has not attracted the attention it deserves. Witty and epigrammatic – one reviewer called it "Mardi Gras on the Eve of Death"[22] – the novel includes a good deal of what Stoppard will put into his plays for the next forty years.

As with *Rosencrantz and Guildenstern Are Dead* – and with numerous subsequent works – Stoppard draws from and builds upon literary predecessors, creating a work, as one reviewer notes, that "is in the fantasist vein and not for every reader. To enjoy it, an absolute literacy, a sense of the absurd, and an ability to lose oneself in nonsense are requisites."[23] Katherine E. Kelly observes that Stoppard adapted some of the characters and narrative strategies from James Joyce's *Ulysses*, "forging his own postmodern epic on the smithy of literary parody."[24] The novel has been compared to works by Kingsley Amis, Evelyn Waugh, P. G. Wodehouse, T. S. Eliot, John Donne, Thornton Wilder, and Voltaire. Influences and comparisons aside – as with *Rosencrantz and Guildenstern Are Dead* – this work is uniquely Stoppardian.

Susan Rusinko puts forward the idea that the two title characters "can be seen as a doppelgänger character, a double torn equally between certainty and doubt."[25] Kenneth Tynan, on the other hand, confesses a suspicion that "Though Stoppard would doubtless deny it, [the] pronouncements of Malquist's have a ring of authority which suggests the author speaking."[26] Tynan may be right to see Stoppard speaking through Malquist, but Tynan's is an impression that can at best be labeled opinion. What we do know is that Lord Malquist and Mr. Moon see the world together but respond to that same world in wildly different ways, each with an insufficiency that undermines his point of view, but each with an appeal that makes it difficult to fully reject either.

Given that the novel is interested in perception and interpretation – as most of Stoppard's works are – it opens with a series of engagingly inscrutable sketches initially left for the reader to muddle into coherence. We hear the well-crafted words of Lord Malquist, a blend of eighteenth-century English courtier and Edwardian dandy, refined, intelligent, obsessed with elegance and style. Moon, just hired to be Malquist's biographer, sits in the lord's coach as it traffics its way through modern-day Whitehall and Mayfair, led on by a stately pair of pigeon-colored horses. Moon listens to Malquist's spontaneous aphorisms while reassuringly patting the time-bomb he keeps in his coat pocket. The coach slips out of control, its black Irish driver not being handy with horses (though he looks good in Malquist's livery), and the coach runs over a woman attempting to deliver a petition through the coach's window. Malquist deals with the incident by tossing coins into the crowd as the coach races on. The coins turn out to be foil-wrapped chocolates.

We also meet Long John (L. J.) Slaughter, rigged out as a cowboy but unable to control his horse, which lopes its way through the city of London heedless of its rider's commands, "Whoa, will ya, whoa boy" (12). His nemesis is Jasper Jones, who has put his spurs on backwards and injures himself whenever he walks. We find out later that he has commercial roots as the "Hungriest Gun in the West man with the porkiest beans straight out of the can" (158). We then watch a woman leave the Ritz Hotel, enter Green Park, lose a shoe, and collapse in a drunken stupor, only to be benignly sniffed over by a male lion, formerly hiding behind a scrub of thorn. Then we meet a dark man, bearded with matted hair and an Irish accent, riding a donkey sidesaddle and wearing a linen robe. The donkey halts at an intersection, causing a massive traffic jam which will inevitably back up to the lord's own accident in the making. Then we enter the bathroom of Jane Moon, sensual, a siren who seems born for pleasure, called "Fertility Jane" by one of the broncs. The two cowboys are fighting for her affections, despite the fact that she's married. Interrupted while "sitting at her toilette" (15), Jane trips into one of her lover's arms because she forgot to pull up her knickers. Though she turns out to be more an exhibitionist flirt than anything else, her free ways and unquestioned sexuality attract everyone, including Lord Malquist, who remains unmoved by passion even as he inspects her navel, weighs her breasts for signs of cancer, and shares the bathroom with her on several occasions. Jane's actions are unchecked by her husband's presence, who feels righteous jealousy but somehow remains unsure that his incredulity and indignation are justified. All of this occurs on the eve of the state funeral of England's last great hero: (the unnamed) Winston Churchill.

The brilliance of Stoppard's quirky menagerie is that it is more than just some ridiculously silly British comedy routine. Stoppard takes this highly unlikely material and turns it into something surprisingly credible, even "normal." The one person who is unable or unwilling to see it all as normal is Moon. These odd bits of cowboys, flirts, and lions are colorful outtakes of a world that Moon, for the life of him, cannot figure out. Forced to deal with the cluttered world around him, Moon's complaint is deep and far-reaching. He is an ethical and honest man – or at least he wants to be – but he is definitely not a strong or heroic man. He is certainly not capable of altering the world around him, but changing the world is not what Moon seems to want. First he bemoans a world where noble ideals have lost their value:

> I don't know a single person who is completely honest, or even half honest, and they don't know it because dishonesty is now a matter of degree, and sincerity is something to be marketed and hunger is a statistic and expediency is god and the white rhino is being wiped out for the racket in bogus aphrodisiacs. (23)

The problem for Moon is the fear that changing the world will have a domino effect that may unintentionally affect innocent millions. It is a fear that sinks Moon into a paralysis of inaction directly reminiscent of T. S. Eliot's Prufrock, to whom Moon frequently alludes. For example, he proposes eliminating automobiles, the scourge of modern society, but the problem is:

> You couldn't stop making them just like that because then there'd be
> hundreds of people out of work, with children and all, and no money
> to spend, so the shopkeepers would get caught up in it, grocers and
> shoeshops and garages and all the people dependent on them, with
> children and all, and if they couldn't go on then the factories and the oil
> refineries would have to stop so there'd be millions of people out of work,
> with children and all.   (19)

Interdependence makes any sort of change virtually impossible because of the
likelihood of cataclysmic results affecting even the most innocent among us. Or
so it appears to Mr. Moon.

Moon crumples under the pressures of sorting out the world around him,
unable to do anything but absorb the overwhelming sense of panic that washes
over him:

> They were all the same fear and he could not even separate the causes.
> He only knew that the source of it all was mass, the feeling of things
> multiplying and expanding, population, buses, buildings, money, all
> interdependent and spreading – a remorseless uncontrollable, unguided
> growth which ballooned around him, refusing to go bang and yet lacking
> the assurance of an infinity.   (42)

But there is more to it than just a feeling that the world is spinning out of control.
Moon is looking for reasons behind this chaos. Everything, surely, has been caused
by some antecedent event. And if this is true, as Moon believes it to be, "Then you
must be prepared to go back to Babylon; because everything connects back, to
the beginning of the history of the world" (69). That is the reason Moon has
decided to write a history of the world: in order to see how everything fits together
in some orderly manner that has escaped him up to this point. For example, it
occurs to Moon "that the labyrinthine riddle of London's streets might be subjected
to a single mathematical formula, one of such sophistication that it would relate
the whole hopeless mess into a coherent logic" (122). Moon wants tight causal
explanations while what he likely should be looking for (judging from Stoppard's
later works) is a sort of logical flexibility which he is not quite capable of grasping.

Though Moon never finds a way out of his existential quagmire, he does
suggest a way to approach the world: "I take both parts . . . leapfrogging myself
along the great moral issues, refuting myself and rebutting the refutation
towards a truth that must be a compound of two opposite half-truths" (53).
Repeated by Stoppard himself in numerous interviews as being his own way of
confronting the world, at its best this dialectical strategy leads to a balanced
understanding of the ways of the world.[27] The problem is that seeing both sides
can also lead to paralysis in thought and action. Paralysis is what happens to

Moon. So while he quietly rages against the world, Moon increasingly realizes that he is ill-equipped to sort out who or what is to blame.

Enter Lord Malquist, sum of virtually everything Moon opposes. If Moon is looking for substance, for concrete reality – or something like that, since he is not exactly certain of what he means by "substance" – then Malquist is the antithesis: "Substance is ephemeral but style is eternal . . . which may not be a solution to the realities of life but it is a workable alternative" (156). Contemplating the funeral of the unnamed Winston Churchill, Malquist gives what could be considered the novel's keynote address:

> His was an age that saw history as a drama directed by great men; accordingly he was celebrated as a man of action, a leader who raised involvement to the level of sacred duty, and he inspired his people to roll up their sleeves and take a militant part in the affairs of the world . . . I think perhaps that such a stance is no longer inspiring nor equal to events – its philosophy is questionable and its consequences can no longer be put down to the destiny of an individual. For this reason, his death might well mark a change in the heroic posture – to that of the Stylist, the spectator as hero, the man of inaction who would not dare roll up his sleeves for fear of creasing the cuffs.   (79)

The scheduled state funeral involves more than burying a single man; it marks the end of an age of great, selfless, and heroic action because the world has gotten too complex for action to have a meaningful effect. This speech explains exactly why Malquist can exclaim without qualm that "I am not frightfully interested in anything, except myself" (68). If action has become irrelevant in the world, Malquist's behavior is a clearly viable option. So goes Stoppard's suggestion.

Stoppard opens the novel by having Malquist basically reveal himself in a shorthand observation that holds true throughout the novel. Speaking to Moon, he offers, "On the day the Bastille fell Louis XVI of France returned home from the hunt and wrote in his private diary, *Rien*. I commend to you the dignity of that remark, not to mention its cosmic accuracy" (8). Moments later Malquist adds: "Nothing . . . is the history of the world viewed from a suitable distance" (8). Style is the lingering residue of civilized existence for Malquist, who chooses to pursue a stylish existence with flawless exuberance. For the reader, Lord Malquist is either admirably or maddeningly irresponsible, utterly ignoring the feelings of others even when he inadvertently commits man-slaughter. We know his lifestyle is unsustainable and parasitic, but Stoppard manages to give this character almost irresistible charisma even as his life choices fly in the face of a traditional, moral, and equitable sense of being. If things will turn out poorly in the end – as they did for Louis XVI – then so be it.

While such stylish aestheticism has its siren-like appeal, Stoppard also highlights that it is "useless" by making Malquist literally impotent, unable and uninterested in procreation, living instead an ethereal existence free from fleshly influences. Malquist notes to Moon, "you probably know that the Malquists in common with other families of equal style and breeding excrete and procreate by a cerebral process the secret of which is passed down in the blood" (67). This ethereality does not sit well with Malquist's wife, who is very much a woman of the flesh, desperate to populate their empty nursery and drowning her emptiness in alcohol. But that is of no concern for Malquist.

Rather, Malquist wants to provide posterity with part of himself first by hiring Moon as his Boswell and having his life of style transmitted as a biography. He is also writing his own book, "a little monograph on *Hamlet* as a source of book titles" (67), a literally superficial topic entirely suited to Malquist. And he shows just a little more than passing envy that certain lords have been immortalized in the vocabulary of the English language. Sandwich is an obvious one, and he notes with scorn that Lord Wellington "wore Malquist boots! . . . He entered the language by appropriating the fruits of my family genius" (9). Wellington may also be remembered as the victor of the Battle of Waterloo, but for Malquist it is the boots that really matter. Malquist admires Sir Wallop, who "so smote the French at sea that he gave a verb to the language" (187). If only Malquist could also enter the English language, his legacy would be set.

Throughout his contact with Malquist, Moon carries with him a bomb and even sets its twelve-hour fuse partway through the novel. The cacophonous disorder that Malquist rises above is exactly what Moon cannot ignore. Population explosions, ever-increasing human suffering, an ever-quickening move toward utter chaos – these large matters obsess Moon: "He felt the shell of human existence ballooning to a thinness that must give way at some point, and his whole nervous system was tensed for the apocalyptic moment. If it did not come soon he would have to anticipate it, in microcosm, for his private release" (19). That is why he plans to use the bomb, to awaken others to the impending apocalypse by presenting a taste of doom in microcosm to the world.

When the moment arrives, however, the bomb comically fails to wreak its carnage, behaving more like a carnival contraption, and Moon is left humiliated and utterly deflated. However, in a strange bit of ironic closure, the man made widower in the beginning of the novel by Malquist's runaway coach mistakes Moon for Malquist and blows poor Moon up with a quite successful bomb. Conscientious Moon dies in apathetic Malquist's place. Much can be made of the point since throughout the novel Moon is cut and sliced about his hands, feet, and face in a pattern that adds up to something similar to the stigmata of Christ. Then he is sacrificed in place of another. Is this bit of symbolism a signal of design, or is seeing this connection merely a curious irrelevance?

Amid the carnage that is Moon, we should recall that Malquist's escapist response is hardly more effective. After all, Malquist's estate is being liquidated by novel's end, offering a harsh reminder that mere aestheticism is not a "real" answer. However, Stoppard leaves us to guess what the consequences of Malquist's bankruptcy might be since the novel ends with Moon's death and not with Malquist's eviction. Malquist does in the end outlive Moon, still on his feet, unconcerned, unruffled.

In a world where, as Moon notes, "reality" is "just outside [our] perception" (32), how we live becomes a matter of grave importance. What Moon knows is that he does not know much, and that is a start. But even though the pursuit of knowledge may rightly be a primary pursuit for humanity, it is a pursuit that does not disqualify style as a pursuit as well. *How we live*, Stoppard and his novel suggest, is a matter of reasonable importance even as we ponder the debatably weightier matter of *why we live*.

Chapter 4

Playing with the stage

There are no consequences to a coat of paint.   *Albert's Bridge* (11)

Several years elapsed between the London premiere of *Rosencrantz and Guildenstern are Dead* (1967) and Stoppard's next full-length play, *Jumpers* (1972). During that hiatus, however, Stoppard was active writing shorter pieces for radio, television, and the stage.

Albert's Bridge was perhaps Stoppard's most notable achievement during this interim period, airing July 13, 1967 on BBC radio shortly after *Rosencrantz and Guildenstern are Dead* opened in London and winning the Prix Italia Award, the most prestigious international radio award of the time. It falls into a growing line of works that feature a central character – a Moon character, basically – utterly confused or repulsed by the way of the world and determined to escape. For example, Gladys in the radio play *If You're Glad, I'll be Frank* (1966) escapes the chaos of life by taking on the job of talking clock for the phone service. John Brown in the television play *A Separate Peace* (1966) retires to an asylum despite being perfectly normal. Albert in *Albert's Bridge* withdraws into what he hopes will be the lifelong career of singlehandedly painting and repainting the Clufton Bay Bridge rather than using his philosophy degree or joining his father in the family business. In addition to the utterly predictable rhythm and order of his job, Albert loves the perspective on the world that he gets from the bridge's heights, feeling much like Lord Malquist who sees order materialize only when viewed from afar. When a miscalculation leaves parts of the bridge exposed and rusting, city planners hire 1,799 workers to paint the bridge in a day. The intrusion destroys Albert's rhythm and happiness, and the weight of the workers catastrophically destroys the bridge itself.

Two one-act plays highlight Stoppard's interest in the technical formalities of theatre production, *The Real Inspector Hound* (1968) and *After Magritte*

(1970). Both were designed, as Stoppard notes, "to bring off a sort of comic coup in pure mechanistic terms."[1] Both take on the task of parody, *The Real Inspector Hound* confronting the Agatha Christie conventions of the whodunit by creating a play about a play about a murder mystery at Muldoon Manor, witnessed by two theatre critics, Moon and Birdboot. Clichés abound in the play-within-a-play as well as in the conversation between the two critics (though Stoppard says "it was never a play *about* drama critics"[2]), who eventually find themselves sucked into the mystery play's deadly action. One critic – the absent Higgs – turns out to be the body found on the stage in the play, Birdboot is shot trying to reveal this fact, and Moon is condemned for his murder, while all along it is the apprentice critic, Puckeridge – disguised as Magnus, the real inspector Hound – who has orchestrated everything in the interest of professional advancement.

Says Stoppard, "I'm very fond of the play because I didn't know how to do it ... I wanted it somehow to resolve itself in a breathtakingly neat, complex but utterly comprehensible way."[3] Even this minor work taps into Stoppard's ongoing interest in the limits of reason. Murder mysteries typically highlight human rational capacities, and audiences often participate by working to solve the mystery before the resolution formally reveals itself. This play is complicated as the boundaries melt away between the Muldoon Manor play and the play occupied by Moon and Birdboot as well as between the critics as audience in a play and the actual audience of the overall production. In addition to asking what is true and false – standard murder mystery fare – we are called on to ask what is reality and what is illusion. Neill Sammells observes, "this 'hall of mirrors' effect criticises that simple model which places art as a reflecting mirror opposite the actuality of life; what is reflected instead is the degree to which life seizes upon the forms of art as a means to self-realisation."[4] Stoppard not only playfully critiques our faith in reason and logic; he also challenges the idea that art holds a mirror up to life, suggesting instead that art influences, interacts, and intertwines with life in ways the mirror metaphor fails to include.

A similar point is made from a different angle in *After Magritte*, which opens with an elderly woman lying on an ironing board, a younger woman in an evening gown on her hands and knees staring down at the floor, and a bare-chested man in fishing waders blowing into an overhead lampshade. What initially looks like a staged version of an absurdist scenario from some surrealist Magritte painting turns out to be perfectly sensible behavior frozen at a comically awkward moment in time. Detective Inspector Foot intervenes, trying to solve a reported robbery involving a one-legged minstrel wearing blackface. Each character recalls witnessing a different culprit, all unusual but all logically plausible. One saw a footballer with a football under his arm, another a man in pajamas holding a tortoise. Another saw an Arab with a gourd, or perhaps a lute or a mandolin. He may have been blind given that he held a white cane, or perhaps it was a closed umbrella. He may have been foaming mad or perhaps had a white beard. He may have been one-legged. The truth eventually bubbles its way to the surface, an Oedipus-like revelation wherein the Inspector discovers he is his own culprit. The mystery in the play is explained, leaving us wondering if perhaps Magritte's own curious art (only casually alluded to in the play) can also be penetrated by logic.

Stoppard's radio play *Artist Descending a Staircase* (1972) includes a title that works much the same way as *After Magritte*, suggesting some connection to Marcel Duchamp's *Nude Descending a Staircase*. What the radio play presents, however, is yet another mystery, this time involving the death of an artist apparently thrown down a staircase. A good deal of artistic debate occupies the play, populated as it is with three opinionated artist friends. This is the play that includes Stoppard's famous epigram, "Skill without imagination is craftsmanship ... Imagination without skill gives us modern art" (19), which on numerous occasions Stoppard has confessed he believes. Abandoning his renowned dialectical back-and-forth, Stoppard has on numerous occasions expressed an unambiguous opinion about the kind of art he prefers, siding with this play's conservative artist Donner: "I think that when Donner says that much modern art is the mechanical expression of a very simple idea which might have occurred to an intelligent man in his bath and be forgotten in the business of drying between his toes, that is me."[5]

The play's structure is itself ingenious, broken into scenes that reverse and advance in time in mirror fashion (A B C D E F E D C B A), beginning with an audio-taped document of the artist's death and ending with the same. But this mechanistic ingenuity serves the larger purpose of encouraging audiences to draw conclusions regarding the apparent murder and then adjust and readjust as more information accumulates. What eventuates is a realization that the dead artist died by accident while trying to strike a buzzing fly. (Allusion to Emily Dickinson's "I heard a Fly buzz – when I died," #465, is surely intended.) The evidence never alters; what alters is the way the living perceive the evidence, audience included. Ingenious in its own right, *Artist Descending a Staircase* gave Stoppard the chance to debate with himself the nature of art before turning to *Travesties* and one of his great comic successes.

In the above as in most of Stoppard's works to follow, perception is re-tooled, mysteries are clarified, and implausibilities are sensibly explained. Characters alternate between fearing and embracing uncertainty, all looking for answers to life's uncertain questions. Using reason as a central tool of comprehension is variously parodied, challenged, and upheld. There seems to be a sense to the universe after all, but it is not necessarily the sort of sense we have previously sought.

Jumpers: not your father's (or mother's) philosophy lesson

> Of all forms of wishful thinking humanism demands the greatest sympathy. *Jumpers* (56)

Jumpers opens with a dazzling but baffling spectacle. It is a political victory party of some sort, and the star attraction is a sultry cabaret singer. The problem is she cannot remember the lyrics for any of the songs she is trying to perform, all of which curiously have something to do with the moon. Almost instantly a trapeze swing cuts across the stage mounted by another beautiful woman who proceeds to do a striptease as the swing swoops in and out of a spotlight. The partygoers go wild. Then a porter with drinks walks on and obstructs the view, unaware that he runs the risk of being crashed into by the trapeze act. The naked lady does finally crash into the porter, ending the entertainment with a bang. Not to be deterred, eight limber but aging gymnasts jump onto the stage and do various stunts. An elderly man enters and complains about the late-night revelry. The singer keeps trying to recollect her lyrics, and the jumpers manage to form a squat pyramid. At the height of the jumpers' accomplishment, however, a gunshot rings out, and one of the jumpers falls out of formation. The pyramid defies gravity for a moment and then collapses. The fallen jumper crawls to the confused singer and dies at her feet leaving blood on her gown. All leave except for the singer, the body, and the honoree of the party, Archie Jumper, leader of the victorious Radical-Liberal Party.

The singer is Dotty. It is her house – shared with her middle-aged husband, philosopher George Moore – and so she is responsible for the body. Archie says he will be back in the morning to clean things up. In her room a television voice is recounting a successful British lunar landing complicated by a damaged craft that will only be able to return one of the two astronauts to earth. News of this lunar event has deeply affected Dotty. Meanwhile, George (the complaining elderly man) has been in his study trying to dictate a lecture he will give tomorrow before a conference of logicians, theologians, and ethicists. The topic is "Man – good, bad, or indifferent?" and George is taking the quixotic position that god, good, and evil are objective realities. Duncan McFee will argue the atheist, radical-liberal relativistic side that argues ethics is a matter of taste and

2 *Jumpers*. The National Theatre, London, 1972

opportunity. In fact, this is the political position that has just swept the Rad-Lib Party into power. The problem is Duncan McFee turns out to be the murdered jumper. Who did it? And what is wrong with Dotty?

Jumpers confirmed that Stoppard was no one-hit wonder, opening in February 1972 in London and transferring to New York in 1974. The play is a major reworking of his 1967 30-minute television play, *Another Moon Called Earth* in which a historian, Bones, is searching for meaningful patterns in human existence (much like Moon's history project in *Lord Malquist and Mr. Moon*) with no luck, while his flirtatious wife Penelope has lost her geocentrist moral center as a result of witnessing the first lunar landing on television, during which her doctor seems to have been taking advantage of his patient. Inspector Crouch enters, announcing the death of a woman, fallen from the apartment building's heights. Nothing is resolved; everything is suggested.

The reworking of this material into *Jumpers* confirms a point Stoppard willingly confesses: "I have enormous difficulty in working out plots, so actually to use *Hamlet*, or a classical whodunit, or another play (which I'm afraid I've just done again [in *Travesties*]) for a basic structure, takes a lot of pressure off me."[6] The changes here are significant, but the echoes between the two plays – as well as other early works – are notable.

The Rad-Libs have won a landslide election victory. It is not clear whether they rigged the election, but for an ethical relativist it does not really matter. And it seems that most of the populace is either indifferent to or actually in favor of the relativist position. Against this tide of popular opinion, George seems to stand alone.

Archie is slick and seductive, polished in every way. His attachment to Dotty is suspicious at best, but every sexual suggestion has a logical and credible explanation. George, on the other hand, is *not* slick. He is a dunderer, well-meaning – his heart seems to be in the right place – but often inadvertently funny. For all the sympathy we may have for George, Stoppard certainly makes it hard to see him as a voice we should respect, follow, and believe.

The murdered Duncan McFee, we find out much later in the play, had a crisis of confidence regarding his Rad-Lib relativism and was on the verge of heading off to a monastery and becoming a St. Paul to George's Jesus, as Archie puts it. Duncan's betrayal of the Rad-Lib cause gives Archie motive for killing him. But Dotty is also a prime suspect because of her brittle condition and onstage opportunity. We find out, too, that Duncan was betrothed to George's secretary, an otherwise coldly professional young woman who also happened to be the trapeze strip-teaser. The problem here is that Duncan was already married. He had already told his wife (another suspect?) but was afraid to tell his mistress. It could be that he told her that night, and in a calculated rage the secretary/mistress killed him.

News reports interrupt the play's action, reporting that two astronauts recently landed on the moon. Complications arise as the two men fight each other for the right to be the only one to return to earth in their damaged craft. This spotlight on selfishness reminded the now-deceased McFee of a recorded act of selflessness involving Captain Robert Scott's doomed 1911 race to the South Pole, when Captain Lawrence Oates altruistically sacrificed himself in the hope that the rest of the party would survive the blizzard that ultimately took all their lives. The thought of Oates's altruism gives McFee all sorts of doubt about his current relativistic, egocentric beliefs, to the point that he tells a friend he is considering suicide. This is another possible explanation for his death, and, though it is suggested, it is highly implausible given the public circumstances of his undoing.

Dotty, we discover, was once a philosophy major who found academic favor with George and eventually married him. She rises in the entertainment world as a torch song wonder. But Dotty is rattled by the fact that humans are on the moon, making this once mysterious and romantic sphere merely another object of human conquest. Furthermore, with men on the moon, universals that humanity pretend to believe in appear to be little more than the local customs of an inconsequential planet in a vast universe.[7] Dotty has become Archie's troubled relativistic acolyte, mouthing such declarations as "Archie says the Church is a monument to irrationality" (26). George is generally undaunted by such declarations, as in this instance: "The National Gallery is a monument to irrationality! Every concert hall is a monument to irrationality! – and so is a nicely kept garden, or a lover's favour, or a home for stray dogs" (26). In fact, concerning the coldly positivist philosophy embraced by Archie, George reminds us that such radical rationalism is only really useful in mundane matters "that can be demonstrated to be true or false, such as that the Bristol train leaves from Paddington" (78). Positivists disqualify anything that is demonstrably unprovable (which is almost everything of real interest) as empty speculation unworthy of serious human consideration.

Through George, Stoppard is confronting a twentieth-century philosophical movement that held serious sway in British intellectual circles for several decades. A. J. Ayer, a man Stoppard got to know quite well in years following the production of *Jumpers*, gets to the heart of positivism in his influential book *Language, Truth, Logic*: "Sentences which simply express moral judgements do not say anything. They are pure expressions of feeling and as such do not come under the category of truth and falsehood."[8] Troubled by the imprecision of feelings and emotions, the positivists argued that facts alone populate the knowable world. From this declaration, it follows that anything failing to be concretely material is presumed simply not to exist. God and morality get caught up in this grand sweep of ontology, along with so much more.

Being a confirmed theist, George must confront positivism and must insist on the limits of rationality, inserting into his lecture "that there is more in me than meets the microscope" (57). And slightly later: "I don't claim to *know* that God exists, I only claim that he does without my knowing it, and while I claim as much I do not claim to know as much; indeed I cannot know and God knows I cannot" (60). This is twisted matter to be sure, and while Stoppard may sympathize with George's position, Stoppard's own stated uncertainty keeps him honest and the debate unresolved: "I've always thought the idea of God is absolutely preposterous but slightly more plausible than the alternative proposition that given enough time, some green slime could write Shakespeare's sonnets."[9]

If reason is somehow an incomplete tool when it comes to understanding our world, we have similar problems when it comes to the senses themselves. Archie uses his medical credentials to inspect a now bed-ridden Dotty, and everything that George sees (and the audience witnesses) seems to indicate an extramarital affair, at least until Archie is given the chance to explain the medical necessity of each action. Everything has a plausible explanation, and what we see could very easily be something other than what we think we see.

Language, too, falls victim to Stoppard's scrutiny. George has anonymously called the police at 2 a.m. to complain about the noise in his living room. The next morning, when Inspector Bones arrives regarding another call – about the murder – George answers Bones's oblique questions by admitting he is the man Bones wants, taking full responsibility for what he did last night and wishing Bones would just overlook this unfortunate incident. Later in the play, George and Crouch the butler blunder in much the same way. Crouch is upset that his friend McFee is dead; George is upset that his rabbit is dead. McFee's body and the rabbit become "it" in conversation, and George tells a horrified Crouch that Dotty is cooking and just now eating "it." Clive James observes that such linguistic confusions are a Stoppard favorite, noting he "is at his strongest when one precise meaning is transformed into another precise meaning with the context full-blown in each case."[10] In these two comic encounters, we get confusion adding to uncertainty.

But there is more. George's lecture brilliantly illustrates the limits of logic when he introduces Zeno's paradoxes, which prove the impossibility of motion, which is of course an absurd thing to prove, and which itself becomes a point that demonstrates the unreliability of logic. If an arrow is shot at a target, before it could reach halfway to its mark it would first have to reach half the distance to the halfway point, and half of that before, etc., until it actually would not move at all, caught up in first needing to reach an infinitely smaller set of points before it could move on to the next point. As a result, "St. Sebastian died of fright" (13).[11] George, however, plans to prove Zeno's logic wrong through the simple empirical act of shooting an arrow, proving the erroneous power of logic. As George is about to fire the arrow, Dotty – desperate for attention in another room – screams "FIRE," shocking George to misfire. (It is an errant arrow that, we find out later, kills Thumper the rabbit.) What we see in George is a man possessed of "common sense" intuition trying to elevate his intuition to objective, rationally verifiable truth. Proof by analogy, not by rational argument, is his only real chance. But while he may succeed at demonstrating the limits of logic, Dotty's intervening scream reminds us of George's real problem.

George, the professed moralist, completely ignores and utterly fails to assist Dotty, a woman – his wife! – in her greatest time of need. Less philosophy in the ivory towers and more field work in your own backyard seems the message. George's obsession to know the world and its rules by locking himself away in his study and pursuing intellectual threads of thought effectively leads him to commit the one genuinely unpardonable sin of the play. George crucially misses every opportunity to prove his humanity and demonstrate the selfless humanistic compassion his philosophy sets up as the highest human ideal. He remains caught up in his study trying abstractly to prove that selflessness is a moral good instead of physically demonstrating his humanity through a simple gesture of human outreach.

If ignoring Dotty's literal cries for help is not problematic enough, in the dreamscape of the play's concluding Coda, George stands by and allows the murder of the new Archbishop of Canterbury, the former Radical-Lib spokesman for agriculture awarded the archbishopric by the new government. When the Archbishop discovers his spiritual side and challenges his new bosses, he suffers martyrdom in a manner akin to Thomas à Beckett while bumbling George stands by in abstracted oblivion.

Then there is the catastrophic mission to the moon which demonstrates Archie's reductionist, amoral vision of the universe with almost petri-dish scientific precision. Seeing the events unfold on the lunar landscape, we are presumably given with crystal clear accuracy an irrefutable proof that self-interest will prevail over moralistic concepts like altruistic self-sacrifice. However, against this gloomy evidence of man's baser natural drives, Stoppard stirs the counterexample into the mix, the recollection of an Antarctic explorer "sacrificing his life to give his companions a slim chance of survival" (70). An apparent case of true altruism leads McFee himself to conclude: "If altruism is a possibility," then his (and Archie's) self-serving philosophy "is up a gum-tree" (70). The Antarctic explorer's altruism surfaces as concrete evidence of a human disposition toward self-sacrifice that undermines Archie's (and McFee's) Hobbesian conclusions about humanity's innate selfishness.

Altruism is, in a word, irrational. Despite that fact, however, humanity holds selflessness up as an ideal, and particular evidence verifies that people quite frequently engage in this most unrewarding of exercises. Why do we commit acts of kindness when, logically speaking, it is such a poor investment of time and energy? Stoppard observes, "This conflict between one's intellectual and emotional response to questions of morality produces the tension that makes the play."[12] It is also the same tension that, irrationally, makes life worth living. Logical positivist A. J. Ayer himself may have best summarized the matter when he observed, "Whatever Kant may have said, morality is very largely founded on sympathy and affection, and for these one does not require religious sanction. Even logical positivists are capable of love."[13]

Travesties: art in an apocalyptic nutshell

> Incidentally, you may or may not have noticed that I got my wires crossed a bit here and there.   *Travesties* (64)

Travesties (1974) is an inside-his-head play. Henry Carr is a British World War I officer whose wounds result in transfer to the diplomatic service and assignment in neutral Zurich, Switzerland, for the remainder of the conflict. But the play is set in the present, and all the onstage events of the past are generated through Carr's memory, including his improbable contacts with Vladimir Ulyanov, soon to be known to the world as Lenin, James Joyce, soon to become the famous author of *Ulysses*, and Tristan Tzara, influential artist of the Dada movement. Stoppard notes of this unusual play topic and delivery strategy: "Joyce, Tzara and Lenin were all in Zurich at the same time. It's not true that they met or were aware of each other's existence. Naturally I had to percolate the whole thing through this man's fallible memory."[14] To this Stoppard attaches another bit of factual information: The historical Carr, it turns out, played a major role in an amateur Zurich production, put on by James Joyce, of Oscar Wilde's *The Importance of Being Earnest*. Carr's dramatic triumph was sullied by failed legal efforts against Joyce to recover the expense of his stage clothing and by Joyce's successful countersuit for the price of tickets Carr sold for his own reimbursement. The overall event left Carr feeling triumphant about the performance but bitter about finances. And years later he receives the ultimate insult of being lampooned in Joyce's *Ulysses*.

Initially it appears that Carr intends his revenge to be *Travesties*. Joyce is portrayed as a poorly dressed, stereotypically penny-pinching Irish tightwad who speaks in limericks (even though he is from Dublin). But Carr loses track along the way, and the play notably turns to larger self-aggrandizing matters. Carr's tentative command of facts is frequently derailed and reconstituted via Carr's recollection of *The Importance of Being Earnest*, complete with mistaken identities, accidentally swapped bundles, absurd love interests, and abounding witticisms. Being in a production appears to be Carr's singular life-triumph, and everything from that point forward seems to filter through that memory.

The dubious virtues of memory are central to the play. As Carr's unreliable memory is given comically free rein to generate dubious recollections, *Travesties* has Carr's memory take on the more serious task of generating a debate on the nature of art, featuring Carr's recollection of the play's lead characters. The

3 *Travesties*. Left to right: John Wood (Henry Carr), Tom Bell (James Joyce). Royal Shakespeare Company/Aldwych Theatre, London, 1974

debate is sophisticated and engaging, suggesting Stoppard's own voice on numerous occasions. For example, from the mouth of Joyce comes a declaration that is undoubtedly Joycean while also suspiciously Stoppardian:

> An artist is the magician put among men to gratify – capriciously – their urge for immortality. The temples are built and brought down around him, continuously and contiguously, from Troy to the fields of Flanders. If there is any meaning in any of it, it is in what survives as art, yes even in the celebration of tyrants, yes even in the celebration of nonentities. What now of the Trojan Wars if it had been passed over by the artist's touch? Dust. A forgotten expedition prompted by Greek merchants looking for new markets. A minor redistribution of broken pots.   (62)

Joyce's reference to broken pots indirectly refers to his nemesis, Tristan Tzara, spokesperson of art-as-vandalism. At the heart of Dadaism is the celebration of civilization's massive turn-of-the-century implosion highlighted by the Great War. Dadaism rather cynically celebrates this catastrophe by practicing an art form demonstrated by Tzara himself: *"smash[ing] whatever crockery is to hand; which done, he strikes a satisfying pose"* (62). When Joyce observes, "Don't you see my dear Tristan you are simply asking me to accept that the word Art means whatever you wish it to mean," Tzara replies, "Why not? You do exactly the same thing with words like *patriotism, duty, love, freedom,* king and country" (39).

Stoppard clearly allows Tzara to counterpunch with effect. Carr's own pro-
nouncement – which basically defends his arch-foe, Joyce – is reminiscent of
Artist Descending a Staircase (and anticipates *The Real Thing*): "An artist is
someone who is gifted in some way that enables him to do something more or
less well which can only be done badly or not at all by someone who is not thus
gifted" (38). Tzara of course disagrees. Cutting up and re-forming Shakespeare's
sonnets is, for Tzara, even more significant than the skilled craft of a conventional
wordsmith because at very least it will not become a tool for reactionary nationalist propaganda.

Between the two men lies Carr's rare vision. Despite his many pedestrian
pronouncements, and even despite some of his more insightful declarations,
Carr's greatest statement on art is the play proper, incubated in his suspect
memory and nurtured by his imagination. Consider the opening scene, one of
Stoppard's typically baffling openings where Joyce, Lenin, and Tzara are all
babbling incomprehensible gibberish. It turns out that Joyce is dictating
abstruse lines from his masterpiece *Ulysses* to his assistant, and Lenin is
dictating in Russian to his secretary. Both turn out to be anything but gibberish.
Tzara's situation, however, is a bit different. He is cutting words on paper into a
hat and then pulling them out and making what he thinks is a nonsense poem.
The joke here, noted by critic Jim Hunter, is that the nonsense English roughly
translates into a French limerick. Tzara's words

> Eel ate enormous appletzara
> Key dairy chef's hat helllearn oomparah
> Ill raced alas whispers kill later nut east,
> Noon avuncular ill day Clara!   (18)

convert in French to:

> Il est un homme, s'appelle Tzara
> Qui des richesses a-t-il nonpareil
> Il reste à la Suisse
> Parce qu'il est un artiste
> 'Nous n'avons que l'arte', il déclara

which roughly translates as:

> He is a man called Tzara
> Who has unparalleled talent
> He stays in Switzerland
> Because he is an artist
> "We have only art," he declared.[15]

Stoppard does not make this revelation easy for his audience, and it is only
the beginning of an array of examples throughout the play where apparent

nonsense reveals an implicit order, even when the apparent nonsense derives from the defender of nonsense himself, as it does in this example.

Even Tzara's arguments are strangely logical. For example, Tzara persistently insists on the meaningless of existence, but he spouts some of the most logical points in the play. For example, arguing with Carr:

> You ended up in the trenches because on the 28th of June 1900 the heir to the throne of Austro-Hungary married beneath him and found that the wife he loved was never allowed to sit next to him on royal occasions; except! when he was acting in his military capacity as Inspector General of the Austro-Hungarian army.   (40)

Tzara uses a causal explanation, which should come from anyone but Tzara. The urge to find/see order is endemic to human consciousness even for Tzara, despite his petulant declaration: "I am sick of cleverness. The clever people try to impose a design on the world and when it goes calamitously wrong they call it fate. In point of fact, everything is Chance, including design" (37). So much is seen to be by design throughout the play that Paul Delaney observes, "*Travesties* more nearly leads us to the conclusion that everything is design, including chance."[16]

Carr's own disheveled mind – and the play, too, as a result – reveals this urge to discover order among disorder. Carr's dramatic "time slips" abound throughout the play, recasting single events as many as five times from different perspectives. And the slips are source for a good deal of the play's hilarity, allowing Stoppard to play with language in ways that do not require audiences to know Russian or French, or even to know the plot of *The Importance of Being Earnest*, though knowing Oscar Wilde's masterpiece certainly enriches the experience: "if society is going to ape the fashions of philosophy, the end can only be ruin and decay" (36). Then there are the vaudevillian exchanges that convey information as they generate humor:

> JOYCE Were there further disagreements between Tzara and
>   Huelsenbeck?
> TZARA There were.
> JOYCE As to?
> TZARA As to the meaning and purpose of Dada.
> JOYCE As indicated?
> TZARA As indicated by manifestoes written by Tzara and those by
>   Huelsenbeck.
> JOYCE Huelsenbeck demanding, for example?
> TZARA International revolutionary union of all creative men and women
>   on the basis of radical Communism – expropriation of property –
>   socialization . . .

JOYCE As opposed to Tzara's demanding?
TZARA The right to urinate in different colors.   (61)

Carr can have Tzara call Joyce a "supercilious streak of Irish puke," and Joyce can call Tzara "an over-excited little man, with a need for self-expression far beyond the scope of your natural gifts" (62). Carr is untethered to character consistency or traditional historicizing, generating retellings that lie somewhere between factuality and fabrication. Crucially, what they reveal is an orderliness that is a credit to Carr's own creative instincts and attendant sense of order.

The play's primary organizing feature is Carr's fond recollection of *The Importance of Being Earnest*, which operates as a prism[17] through which everything is richly altered into a fable of unlikely happy endings. Virtually everything in Carr's consciousness finds its filter through his recollection of that production.

All is not light and airy, however. Interrupting this fantastic sleight of theatre, and always at least in the background, are Lenin and his assistant Cecily. After a brilliantly crafted and comically ingenious first act, Stoppard opens the second act with a Leninist lecture presented by Cecily. Stoppard almost perversely disappoints audience expectations with an intentionally tedious, entirely "artless" second-act-opening history lesson. In act one Cecily is set up as the charming but limited librarian intent on learning about the world by reading the encyclopedia from A to Z. She becomes Lenin's acolyte, and opens act two by reading verbatim from an actual Lenin speech, revealing Lenin's limited, restrictive vision of order that is determined not to allow art to do anything more than to propagandize his agenda.[18] Ironically, but never stated in the play, Lenin advocates exactly what Tzara and Joyce together most abhor about art: the danger of having it co-opted for a cause. But the play eventually pushes Lenin into the shadows, returns to its festive frolic, and falls into an exuberant celebration of improbable resolutions straight from Oscar Wilde's bag of theatrical tricks.

Following the comic resolution, the play's end arrives with disturbing factuality. Carr, it turns out, is not who he claims to be. Carr turns out to have been a minor bureaucrat, unimportant and unsuccessful in attaining the full life of glamor and import he dreams about. But his imaginative recollections, in the form of *Travesties* itself, have managed to convert the dull lead of his life into the rich ore of art. Carr may have travestied Wilde's masterpiece, travestied Joyce, Tzara, and history in general, but through those travesties Carr transformed his life to art. Reflection, engagement, fabrication – and skill – are cornerstones of the artistic enterprise. Observation and report at best play supporting roles.

Night and Day: journalism in the shadows

> All facts and no news.   *Night and Day* (20)

Following his two highly theatrical farce masterpieces, Stoppard turned to the basically anti-theatrical form of realism in his next work, *Night and Day* (1978). It is a play more in line with the serious British theatre scene of the time, and it feels far less Stoppardian than his previous successes.

But, much as he did with *Enter a Free Man*, Stoppard does not simply subscribe to the realist format as is; he works to stretch matters by confusing "real" scenes with dream sequences, splitting main characters into two, and utilizing interior monologue. And while the play does step into the realm of socially relevant realist critique, it gets a Stoppardian reworking, resulting in a firm challenge to standard liberal views on journalism, unions, and freedom of speech. To complicate matters, Stoppard entangles a love affair into the issues at hand. It should also be added that though *Night and Day* includes a good deal of Stoppardian wit, it is not one of his signature "funny" plays. Of the major plays, perhaps only *Hapgood* is less funny.

The fictional African country of Kambawe, following liberation from British colonial rule, is now approaching civil war between an authoritarian government and a power-hungry insurgent opposition. The play is set in the home of a British colonial business magnate who is able to guarantee wealth to whichever side winds up controlling the country. His wife is an attractive, intelligent woman bored by her life. Several European journalists converge on the house in anticipation of getting a scoop[19] on the unfolding political drama. What ensues is a debate about journalistic rights and privileges, free press in general, colonialism and its transgressions, and love and sex. All comes to a head when it is reported that one of the journalists has been killed and one of the surviving journalists will not be able to have his scoop published because of a writers' strike back home, an action he vocally supported throughout the play.

The play uses theatre in several very lively ways, letting us know at the beginning that this is Stoppard's theatre. The play opens with the deafening approach of a helicopter, generating a wind storm and warping the set's tropical foliage. Shadows of the copter's blades cut strobe-like across the stage's lighting. A jeep then crashes through the foliage, headlights beaming into the auditorium, spotlights crossing everywhere until they settle on the jeep. Deafening machine-gun fire follows. The driver jumps out, jeep vanishes, driver screams out (barely heard amid the din) "Press! Press!" But the spotlight catches him, and a machine-gun burst strikes him down.

Instantly the scene changes. The "driver," Guthrie, is in a garden chair, just waking up to the rat-a-tat-tat of a telex machine. Despite the vividness of it all, it has only been a dream. The audience is left wondering: Was that somehow a recollection of an actual event, or was his mind just making it up? Does Guthrie look at his world from the macho heroic point of view we see him dreaming about? Does his point of view cloud his reporting? From there we can turn to the play proper and begin to focus on how reliable journalistic reports can be if they are filtered through such vivid imaginations.

Stoppard continues to unsettle his audience with an assault on language. Guthrie meets Ruth, the wife of the manor, and Guthrie tells her that "the boy let me in" (40). Ruth smartly notes, "By the way, we don't call them 'boy' anymore" (5), a proper, "liberal" response. Unfazed, Guthrie replies, "Boy about this high, fair hair, your mouth, knows about cameras . . . . His name's Alastair" (6). He is describing Ruth's son. It is not just a matter of what we see that will come into question within the play, it is also a matter of how what we see should be put into words. Journalism strives for an objectivity that Stoppard believes is impossible. The point is nothing new in Stoppard's theatre, but in this play he confronts it head-on.

Ruth's husband Geoffrey is a successful colonial businessman who hopes to continue his success following the postcolonial transition. His home is equipped with all the European conveniences, including the telex machine that attracts the British journalists to his home, the fastest and most reliable means of contact with the outside world. Amid such high stakes, journalism reveals itself to be wildly free-wheeling, requiring adrenalin-pumping bravado and a good deal of luck in order to succeed.

Milne, a relatively green reporter, has just gotten the scoop of the week, an interview with the rebel leader after having found his way into the rebel stronghold. The other journalists, clearly envious, wonder why his report was given the anonymous byline, "From a special correspondent." They eventually learn that Milne refused to support a strike back home and is therefore a scab for whom no journalist has any respect. When found out, Milne defends himself in a manner that sounds a bit like Stoppard himself speaking:

> As soon as they started trying to get me to join the strike it was as if their brains had been taken out and replaced by one of those little golf ball things you get in electric typewriters ... "Betrayal" ... "Confrontation" ... "Management" ... My God, you'd need a more supple language than that to describe an argument between two amoebas. (31)

The strike occurred shortly after the printer's union won a deal that would pay printers more than journalists. When the strike was settled, Milne refused union terms because the terms included a "closed shop" working agreement. A man of principle, Milne resigned because he believed that a closed shop among journalists undermines freedom of speech.

Others, Wagner and Guthrie included, argue that the rich keep getting richer, "and nothing's going to change that without worker solidarity" (33). But Milne points out that this solidarity against management overlooks the more insidious byproduct of needing to join a journalistic club before being able to publish. Wagner and Guthrie will hear nothing of this sort of talk.

Ruth Carson is both an anomaly – not being a journalist – and a crucial addition to this play about a seemingly objective enterprise engulfed in masculine hubris. Ruth reveals she has had bad previous contacts with the media in the form of scandalmongers in London and, more personally, in the form of a recent, brief affair with Wagner in London. When they re-meet here in her home, Wagner calmly asks Geoff and Ruth to call him Dick. Ruth says "I'm not terribly fond of Dick," to which Wagner replies straight-faced: "You could have fooled me" (39). From Wagner, the low comment is not a surprise, and Ruth remains the civil hostess she is expected to be. But here Stoppard does something against the norm of realist expectations by allowing Ruth to articulate her thoughts by way of a body double, "Ruth." Where Ruth must simply hold her tongue, "Ruth" enters the fray and says what Ruth feels but cannot voice: "Get out of this house! This is no longer Geoffrey Carson's bachelor's quarters ... and I'm sick of all you hooligans playing bicycle polo in my sitting room" (44–45). Of course, it all falls on deaf ears, at least onstage.

Having this living reminder of a sexual liaison show up at her house puts Ruth in an awkward situation. She reflects – in a curiously Stoppardian manner: "A lady, if surprised by melancholy, might go to bed with a chap, once; or a thousand times if consumed by passion. But twice... *twice*... a lady might think she'd been taken for a tart" (54). Having Ruth in the play certainly livens it up quite a bit, especially if it is someone like Diana Rigg (the original Ruth) luring us in with talk like, "I was meant to be one of those women who halt the cutlery as they pass through hotel dining rooms on the first night of the holiday... tits-first to the table through the ack-ack of teeny-weeny diamond engagement rings" (51). But there is more to her character than that.

This near-the-surface sexuality takes centerstage as Stoppard brings the naive but dynamic and attractive Milne to Ruth's attention. The idealistic Milne waxes almost poetic when he insists, "A free press, free expression – it's the last line of defense for all the other freedoms" (63). And as he says that "Dick wants union membership to be a license to practice" (64), "Ruth" tries to calm Ruth down with "Watch yourself Tallulah" (64) and then with "This party's looking up – who's this rather interesting young man?" (65). Ruth is clearly falling for Milne, who continues with his speech on free press: "No matter how imperfect things are, if you've got a free press everything is correctable, and without it everything is concealable" (65). Act one ends with Milne and Guthrie going off to an interview.

Act two opens with the two men returning and Ruth/"Ruth" seducing Milne. Eventually Ruth succeeds, and Milne and Ruth/"Ruth" retire to a back room in the house. Almost immediately Ruth re-enters and asks for a cigarette from her husband who has walked into the room. The seduction scene, it turns out, is another act-opening dream scene. In reality, Milne is still out with Guthrie, and Geoff is up late waiting for someone, presumably Milne and Guthrie. The audience has been manipulated once again, in an instance that captures the sensationalism appeal of tabloid, one of the aspects of the profession that the play speaks against, even though it does increase circulation, and even though – ironically – it adds luster to the play proper.

In actuality, Geoff stays home waiting for President Mugeeba to arrive, and a lingering Wagner smells an exclusive interview. Mugeeba arrives. We learn that he has a London School of Economics education, though he says, "It has proved to be a great handicap" (86) as he pursues his own nationalist agenda. Though he is freed from colonial shackles, he realizes he still needs colonial

4 *Night and Day*. Left to right: Diana Rigg (Ruth Carson), Olu Jacobs (President Mageeba), John Thaw (Dick Wagner). Phoenix Theatre, London, 1978

technology and expertise. The discussion fills with propagandistic observations about the good of the country, etc., but the real turn occurs when Wagner and Mugeeba begin talking about British newspapers and the free press. Mugeeba sees the press as the mouthpiece of a few European millionaires, arguing eloquently against management, but also against the current collective bargaining system.

Ruth steps into the conversation, and hiding her opinion by claiming it is her son's, points out that the free press argument confuses "freedom with capability" (97). Freedom grants everyone the right to express himself, but only wealth allows a person to maximize the freedom by giving him the means to distribute his thought. Mugeeba closes the lively debate by listing all the ills of a free press – including letting traitors have a voice and lying about the truth as the government sees it – and says his country's press is free but will be edited by a relative. In a growing rage, he expresses himself by striking Wagner with his cane, at which moment a jeep arrives with a winded Guthrie.

Mugeeba's army, apparently, is just a band of ruffians, and they attacked Guthrie's jeep without provocation, killing Milne in the process. Guthrie is outraged, but he does have a photo essay to get back to London. Then in a twist that requires the timing of an old-fashioned melodrama, the telex machine spits out a message informing all that the unions have shut down the newspapers and there is no rush to transmit any news items after all. "Wotwu" cuts through the message: "Workers of the world unite" (110). Pro-union men Guthrie and Wagner lose their scoop because of local politics back home. Information, truth, news take back seats to business and control of the industry. Ironically, both men will continue working on the fast-breaking events surrounding them even though they are supposed to obey a work stoppage. Ruth and Wagner close the play with Wagner asking Ruth if she had a thing for Milne. The scene and play end with Wagner at the piano and "Ruth" singing "The Lady is a Tramp."

Stoppard's mixing of low and high, sex and politics, local and international affairs is a strategy that will find more successful fusions in later works. Looking back on *Night and Day* in 2008 and reflecting on his opposition to union control of the media via closed-shop legislation, Stoppard shows his continued willingness to leap-frog his own ideas, observing: "Now I'd be capable of writing a letter in reply to myself ... Look at Berlusconi and Putin – it's complete manipulation and control."[20]

Chapter 5

Science takes the stage

The future is disorder.   *Arcadia* (48)

With *Hapgood* (1988) and *Arcadia* (1993), Tom Stoppard consciously mined advances in contemporary science and crafted those advances into a uniquely Stoppardian brand of stageworthiness. It is important to note, however, that even before 1988 Stoppard demonstrated an interest in the sciences, a point noted by Clive James, who concluded as far back as 1975 that "the appropriate analogies" throughout Stoppard's career "lie just as much in modern physics as in modern philosophy."[1] Many earlier works ingeniously warp time and space, while others suggest a budding chaotics paradigm at work. A voracious reader of science texts, Stoppard even credits James D. Watson's *The Double Helix: A Personal Account of the Discovery of DNA* with providing him a description of his writing process.[2]

With *Hapgood* and *Arcadia*, science plays a central and conspicuous role, even to the point of drawing from clearly identifiable sources. Katherine E. Kelly observes that significant portions of dialogue by Kerner, *Hapgood*'s resident quantum physicist, derive directly "from *The Feynman Lectures on Physics*, especially those in chapter 37, 'Quantum Behavior.'"[3] And for *Arcadia*, Stoppard acknowledges a debt to James Gleick's popular *Chaos: Making a New Science*.[4] Stoppard has a son who was a student of physics during this period, which may also in part explain this interest.[5] Clearly, though, *Hapgood* is Stoppard's first play overtly utilizing ideas culled from contemporary science for thematic as well as structural purposes.[6]

Hapgood: now you see me, now you don't

> One thing led to another until causality was dead.   *Hapgood* (49)

Hapgood is, as one reviewer summarizes, "part Feydeau farce, part LeCarré, part science lecture and metaphysical conundrum."[7] The play is in particular what Stoppard's works are in general – a staged thought experiment in the manner Kelly directly outlines: "Act 1 leads to a hypothesis; act 2 carries out the experiment. The denouement leaves to us the interpretation of the results."[8] The hypothesis involves the nature of human behavior, testing whether human "agents" (as used in espionage *and* in science) are irreducibly discrete entities or are phenomena that can indeterminately behave in ways simulating quantum behavior.

The play begins with a voice-over "radio play" detailing agent movements with cool certainty. But upon the opening of the play proper, everything becomes hopelessly muddled. Agents enter and exit changing-room stalls, depositing and exchanging briefcases in a human shell game that is quite literally impossible to follow. After what amounts to a blown assignment by British and American agents, the British leader Hapgood and her crew enter and conclude that the only solution to this shell game had to be that there were two identical Russian agents posing as a single agent. We later discover that two sets of twins – not just one set – were at work.

Kerner, the double agent and physicist who is the center of attention in this espionage matter, reveals that the shell game presented in this first scene amounted to a reproduction of a centuries-old puzzle involving the bridges of Königsberg (the home of philosopher Immanuel Kant): "An ancient amusement of the people of Königsberg was to try to cross all seven bridges without crossing any of them twice" (45). What finally was concluded was, "It can't be done, you need two walkers" (46). Kerner says the shell game that opened the play "was the bridges of Königsberg, only simpler" (46).

Kerner also serves as the play's science guide, explaining the basic tenets of quantum mechanics by relating "the case of the experiment with the two holes."[9] If subatomic material (i.e., light) is shot through two holes and against a light-sensitive recording device, a wave pattern will form on that backdrop, revealing that material is functioning holistically like a wave. However, if we closely "watch" the material as it is being shot through the two holes, the material will generate particle patterns, revealing that this same material is now behaving like particles passing discretely through the two separate holes. Kerner is describing something that is, of course, entirely counterintuitive and seems in fact surely false. But he is accurately describing the strange particle behavior that is the cornerstone of quantum physics. The crucial point is that in the subatomic world, two sets of characteristics – wave and particle behavior – can simultaneously inhere in the same entity. The related key point is, as Kerner observes, "Every time we don't look we get wave pattern. Every time we look to see how we get wave pattern, we get particle pattern. The act of observing determines the reality" (12).

Applying these abstractions to the world of personal human existence, Kerner pulls everything together by connecting espionage to quantum physics:

> The particle world is the dream world of the intelligence officer. An electron can be here or there at the same moment. You can choose; it can go from here to there without going in between; it can pass through two doors at the same time, or from one door to another by a path which is there for all to see until someone looks, and then the act of looking has made it take a different path … It defeats surveillance because when you know what it's doing you can't be certain where it is, and when you know where it is you can't be certain what it's doing.   (48)

The play has effectively moved away from the opening-scene twinning conundrum and on to the idea that one person/agent can be seen simultaneously two different ways. Observer prejudice determines how X is (are?) seen, and Kerner is a perfect case in point. He is both physicist and secret agent, by heritage German and Russian (having been born in the German city of Königsberg which became Russian after World War II and was renamed Kaliningrad), by current affiliation both Russian and British (working for both governments), by inclination an artist though by training a scientist, fluent in both Russian and English, lover and employee of Hapgood (and the father of her son). He is not logically either/or but counterintuitively both/and.

The official job for Blair and Hapgood is to determine which of each of the oppositions Kerner actually is, but the fact that he is *both* defeats Blair and Hapgood before they even begin. Trained to exercise rational, objectivist deduction, Blair and Hapgood refuse to accept simultaneous conjunctions of any of these qualities. They are very good at what they do and rise to standards of intelligence (in both senses of the word) that far exceed traditional expectations. Hapgood demonstrates her singular rational grasp of reality through "the grid," a tool of logic which she uses with precision in her work and in personal life as well, for example by helping her son at school find a missing key. Her mind is so well organized that she can play chess from memory. Even more rigorously logical than Hapgood (though far less imaginative), Blair is entirely dedicated to the "technical," at the expense of any distraction that might be considered "personal." The logic of excluded middle – that everything must be either/or – formally rules both of their professional lives, as Kerner points out in conversation with Blair: "You have been too long in the spy business, you think everybody has no secret or one big secret, they are what they seem or they are the opposite ... If only you could figure it out like looking into me to find my root ... We're all doubles. Even you ... [W]e're not so one-or-the-other" (72).

Through the course of the play, despite their initial sets of similarities, it emerges that Hapgood and Blair are fundamentally different. Hapgood's icon-oclasm surfaces with entertaining frequency, revealing breaks from linear and rational professionalism that Blair will never allow himself to indulge. While Kerner is a center of attention for a great deal of the play, Hapgood's conversion to Kerner's way of thinking makes it to centerstage during the latter part of the play. And coming to grips with twinning is what forces Hapgood's conversion.

The actual twinness of the two Russians in the opening scene first directs us toward the idea of doubling. But the play moves quickly to the kinds of doubling that extend beyond mere biological twinning. So while we come to learn that the other twins – the two Ridleys – succeeded at carrying out counterespionage plans in Athens, Paris, and now in London, the one Ridley we get to know (rather than his unstaged twin) quickly becomes the central subject of interest as the focus shifts to matters of twinning within a single skin. Ridley has grown to see the whole espionage enterprise as a useless game (recalling Purvis in *The Dog It Was That Died*), a conclusion that allows his personal side to invade his technical or professional side. He reveals two sides within his one self and begins to confuse the two. Concerning the secret plans that may cost Hapgood her son's life if they are not handed over to the Russians, Ridley suggests:

> Why don't we just give it to them [the Russians]? What does it matter? ... [A] kid like that, he should be in bed anyway, we can all get some sleep ... Are we talking about a list of agents in place? Are we talking about blowing the work names? The batting order in Half Moon Street? Any of those and all right, the boy maybe has to take his chances. But what has Kerner got? (*Derisively*) The solution to the anti-particle trap. Since when was the anti-particle trap a problem?   (59)

Ridley allows his personal to invade his technical side in ways similar to Kerner's own quantum-like double agency, given that Kerner likely helped the Russians after they discovered that Joe is Kerner's (and Hapgood's) son. But Ridley is finally unable to integrate this seemingly schizophrenic behavior in the same ways that Kerner is. He is ultimately two discrete Ridleys occupying one body, muddling his affairs by remaining in the realm of either/or (as either an agent for Russia or for Britain) rather than a quantum-like both/and agent. And Ridley reveals another level of muddle when he speaks of Hapgood: "I'll get her kid back for her but it's only personal. If she sets me up I'll kill her" (82). Ridley is unable to operate *both* as a government/technical agent *and* as a personal friend. Ridley cannot occupy two worlds simultaneously. Kerner, on the other hand, understands the nature and consequences of doubling, enfolding his multiple selves into a seamless singular whole.

Unlike Ridley (or Blair), Hapgood willingly learns from Kerner. Signs are everywhere that she sits on the verge of such a conversion: while undercover and incognito, she sends postcards to her son Joe, uses secret technology to communicate with a chess opponent in Canada, and uses the red phone in her office – a direct line to Downing Street – to call her son at school. She cherishes the nickname "mother" in her job and is a mother who equally cherishes sharing secret business practices with her son.

Actual, clinical schizophrenia is of course not the subject of this play, though Stoppard does build on Hapgood's schizophrenic existence by having her actually play her own twin in the sting operation that catches Ridley(s). The Hapgood alter ego is a scattered, profane opposite of the agent/mother Hapgood, a part of Hapgood's self she seems thus far to have successfully subdued. Hapgood, in undercover disguise as her own twin, describes her different selves to Ridley: "Well, she was the scholarship girl and I was the delinquent. Having the kid was good for her, she always thought the delinquents had the bastards and the scholarship girls had the wedding. It shook up her view of the world, slightly" (77). This self-analysis may be the first time Hapgood has allowed herself to express such thoughts about her rebel side, rather surprisingly revealing a more complete and complex – even contradictory – person in the process.

As a result, Hapgood realizes that the irreconcilable personal and technical in their broadest reaches counterintuitively constitute some singular whole of her existence. Now that she understands the full scope of what has been nothing short of counter-rational behavior on her part, perhaps she can more successfully and more consciously satisfy inclinations with behavior that is guiltlessly inconsistent. Cohesion of being is not singularly linear but multiple and simultaneous. Even as we strive to generate a majority self for public (or even personal) consumption, there's something to be said for acknowledging the quantum selves that stride side-by-side with the selves we choose to show the world.

With *Hapgood*, Stoppard experiments with quantum mechanics to hypothesize a vision of human behavior that is far more complex than typically envisioned. With Hapgood Stoppard creates a full-blooded character who develops a more complete sense of how the world operates by accepting the quantum model of uncertain behavior and simultaneous being. Much of that same sense of uncertainty is celebrated in his next work, with far greater popular and critical success.

Arcadia: with a world like this, heaven can wait

> It's the best possible time to be alive, when almost everything you thought you knew was wrong. *Arcadia* (49)

A bright, curious, but sheltered young girl asks her tutor the meaning of "carnal embrace." He replies, off-handedly, that carnal embrace involves "throwing one's arms around a side of beef" (1). *Arcadia* is in many ways an extended discussion of these opening lines. It is a discussion that shares space with myriad other discussions, but all of them seem to return to the disorienting nature of sex and love in a world theoretically governed by reason. *Arcadia* is set in 1809, which is a time when nineteenth-century British romantic poets and philosophers were working to separate themselves from the eighteenth-century Age of Reason, calling into question whether the mind or the heart would prevail as *the* way of looking at the world. To this world Stoppard adds "the present-day," set on the same British country estate but with nearly two hundred years separating them. Not surprisingly, the twentieth-century folks are just as torn between whether the head or the heart should prevail.

  Arcadia draws from numerous influences. Thomas Love Peacock's nineteenth-century novel *Headlong Hall* may have influenced Stoppard's decision to use landscape architecture as a way to illustrate the changing world of early nineteenth-century England. Lord Byron's letters and diaries were also works of interest. What may have particularly interested Stoppard was that Byron's daughter Ada was a mathematics prodigy, a perfect model for Stoppard's own prodigy Thomasina. Lindsay Clarke's 1989 novel *The Chymical Wedding* appears to be Stoppard's source for a modern researcher trying to recover the life of a reputed female genius killed in a fire in the early 1800s. A. S. Byatt's 1990 novel *Possession* is a detective story that is set in both contemporary and historical England. Louise Page's 1991 play *Adam was a Gardener* moves between present and past as well, and utilizes landscape gardening as a central motif. For the science in *Arcadia*, Stoppard drew heavily from James Gleick's immensely popular 1987 book *Chaos: Making a New Science*, an accessible though still challenging work on a wide variety of scientific disciplines that loosely falls under the heading "chaos theory."

And Benoit Mandelbrot's *The Fractal Geometry of Nature* popularized the concept of fractals that likely further influenced Stoppard.

Arcadia pointedly utilizes chaos theory in ways that his other plays, both earlier and later, obliquely and perhaps unconsciously touch upon. Chaos theory identifies the balance between order and disorder that generates our universe's vast diversity and even creates conditions suitable for life itself. Chaos theory, as Stoppard reports through his character Valentine, is a theory that revolutionizes our understanding of "[t]he ordinary-sized stuff which is

5 *Arcadia*. Directed by Trevor Nunn. Design:
Mark Thompson. Lighting: Paul Pyant. Standing: Bill Nighy (Bernard Nightingale); Samuel West (Valentine Coverly), Felicity Kendal (Hannah Jarvis). Lyttelton Theatre/National Theatre, London, 1993

our lives" (48). This is a key point because chaos theory is unlike those two other twentieth-century revolutions, relativity and quantum physics, which Valentine reminds us only "explain the very big and the very small" (48). Relativity describes strange universal goings-on like black holes, while quantum mechanics explains equally strange happenings at the subatomic level. Chaos theory, however, describes the world where we live.

Ingeniously, Stoppard suggests a connection between twentieth-century chaos theory and early nineteenth-century British romanticism. The common bond between the two is that they both challenge the "neoclassical" eighteenth-century view of the world as orderly, logical, and unchanging. Very specifically, Stoppard has the young Thomasina of the nineteenth-century world grasp the significance of her own growing skepticism toward an order inspired by Newtonian physics when she properly evaluates an obscure text actually from the period ("A prize essay of the Scientific Academy in Paris") and concludes that the text "contradicts determinism" (81). She in turn applies an "equation of the propagation of heat in a solid body" (81) to Noakes's steam engine (the one working on the estate) and essentially discovers the second law of thermodynamics, or entropy. As Thomasina rightly concludes, in rather simple yet profound terms, if you stir a bowl of rice pudding and jam, "the spoonful of jam spreads itself round making red trails like the picture of a meteor in my astronomical atlas. But if you stir backward, the jam will not come together again. Indeed, the pudding does not notice and continues to turn pink" (4–5). Thomasina's demonstration is Stoppard's apt illustration of irreversible entropic dissipation. Hence, Thomasina discovers that Newtonian laws are incomplete at best. Furthermore, by demonstrating that, as her tutor Septimus Hodge later concedes, "atoms do not go according to Newton" (81), Thomasina realizes how thoroughly her budding thermodynamic ideas challenge Newtonian determinism. Things do not happen as Newton proposed, at least not all (or even most) things. Complexity must be ignored for Newtonianism to succeed. Stoppard's Thomasina, growing up in a world increasingly uncertain about eighteenth-century order, is revolutionary in her understanding of the world around her.

While thermodynamics gets a certain degree of attention in the play, it is only a starting point in an agenda that includes an extended visit to the romantic period of the early nineteenth century. To clarify its tenets, Stoppard sets up a contrastive paradigm between the classical gardening styles of the eighteenth century and the romantic/Gothic picturesque wildernesses that would overtake classical formalism. The proposed conversion of the grounds at the country estate Sidley Park[10] are described by Lady Croom, the resistant lady of the manor:

> Here [in a sketch] is the Park as it appears to us now, and here [in another sketch] as it might be when Mr. Noakes has done with it. Where there is the familiar pastoral refinement of an Englishman's garden, here is an eruption of gloomy forest and towering crag, of ruins where there was never a house, of water dashing against rocks where there was neither spring nor a stone I could not throw the length of a cricket pitch. My hyacinth dell is become a haunt for hobgoblins, my Chinese bridge, which I am assured is superior to the one at Kew, and for all I know at Peking, is usurped by a fallen obelisk overgrown with briars –.   (12)

Irregularity prevails in the picturesque style, drawing from the unfettered spirit of rising romanticism.

It is irregularity in nature that Thomasina pursues in her iconoclastic studies. She glowingly calls Noakes "The Emperor of Irregularity" (85) and sees his landscaping work as the inspiration for her "New Geometry of Irregular Forms" (43). Caught up in the excitement of new discoveries, Thomasina says she "will start with something simple," picks up an apple leaf and declares she will find a way to "plot" it "and deduce its equation" (37). Thomasina's "Geometry of Irregular Forms" is essentially fractal geometry, though without the help of a computer (or perhaps a dedicated hermit) her insights will never bear practical fruit because literally millions of calculations must be made (via algorithmic iteration) before any sense can be made of the calculations. The results – if enough calculations are made and if the algorithm is meaningful – will duplicate on paper the structure of naturally occurring objects such as leaves, rivers, and arterial systems in animals. Benoit Mandelbrot explains the situation, speaking in terms Thomasina would understand:

> Clouds are not spheres, mountains are not cones, coastlines are not circles, and bark is not smooth, nor does lightning travel in a straight line … [C]ompared with *Euclid* [i.e., standard geometry] … Nature exhibits … an altogether different level of complexity. The existence of these patterns challenges us to study those forms that Euclid leaves aside as being "formless," to investigate the morphology of the "amorphous."[11]

Fractal geometry uncovers an order in nature that previous ordering systems have been too limited to recognize. What is important is the surprising self-similarity that nature utilizes, not precisely duplicative and therefore confusing to more rigid ways of trying to see order in the world. While more formal systems of thought see only frightful arrays of disorder in nature, fractal geometry in particular and chaos theory in general have uncovered levels of relatively simple order amid complexities previously written off as "random" or "chaotic."

It is important to note that Stoppard's Thomasina is not necessarily a curious anachronism that Stoppard whimsically invented for the stage. Goethe (1749–1832), the famous nonfictional contemporary of Thomasina, contemplated precisely the same things she does. Goethe's studies led him to the notion of an *Urpflanze*, or original plant, from which, he argued, all other plants are morphologically derived. It is an idea that went largely unregarded, as Bohm and Peat observe in *Science, Order and Creativity*, "Because most of the prevailing ideas concerning the development of form were, at that time, expressed in terms of Euclidian geometry and sequential order, Goethe's notion found little resonance in the science of his day."[12] Thomasina, too, complains that the current mathematics that she is being taught produces "equations [which] only describe the shapes of manufacture" and that if this is God's mathematics, then "God could only make a cabinet" (37). Her tutor Septimus, brilliant but Cambridge-educated and therefore fundamentally Newtonian/Euclidean, replies that God "has mastery of equations which lead into infinities where we cannot follow," to which Thomasina replies, "What a faint heart. We must work outward from the middle of the maze" (37). She chooses to assume a mastery which will reveal God's mystery to her.

Indeed, while Thomasina's perspective encourages a widening view of the idea of order in existence, the actual cultural perspective of her contemporaries argues that God is indeed a Newtonian. When Lady Croom nearly apostrophizes her park, she essentially makes just this connection:

> The slopes are green and gentle. The trees are companionably grouped at intervals that show them to advantage. The rill is a serpentine ribbon unwound from the lake peaceably contained by meadows on which the right amount of sheep are tastefully arranged – in short it is nature as God intended, and I can say with the painter, "*Et in Arcadia ego!*" "Here I am in Arcadia." (12)[13]

The delusion is obvious. Nature has been regularized to conform to a human vision of what God's creation should be: orderly, linear, geometrically symmetrical. Irregularity is deemed unnatural and clearly not part of God's true design. The reality, of course, is that nature uncontrolled does not produce such regularity (despite human wishes); rather, it obeys fractal necessity, irregularity created by an "order" that allows small points of deviation to effect an infinity of self-similar opportunities. Thomasina does not accept her mother's Arcadia, looking instead for an expanded vision and encouraging nature to reveal its own orderly though irregular design.

Stoppard introduces the late twentieth-century counterparts alongside the nineteenth-century cast, including Valentine, the student of nonlinear

6 *Arcadia*. Directed by David Leveaux. Set design:
Hildegard Bechtler. Costumes: Amy Roberts. Lighting: Paul Anderson.
Ed Stoppard (Valentine Coverly), Samantha Bond (Hannah Jarvis).
Duke of York's Theatre, London, 2009

mathematics who provides regular commentary on the chaotics nature of existence. He comments directly on news that Thomasina was trying to graph a leaf: "If you knew the algorithm and fed it back say ten thousand times, each time there'd be a dot somewhere on the screen. You'd never know where to expect the next dot. But gradually you'd start to see this shape, because every dot will be inside the shape of this leaf" (47). Valentine describes unpredictable patterns as pervasive in nature: "It's how nature creates itself, on every scale, the snowflake and the snowstorm" (47). And later, from size to time, he describes scale in weather patterns: "Six thousand years in the Sahara looks like six months in Manchester, I bet you" (48). Apparent patternlessness becomes orderly when scale is considered. Valentine concludes rather straight-forwardly, "The unpredictable and the predetermined unfold together to make everything the way it is" (47), a commonplace observation among chaos scientists today but the very thing Thomasina was groping to conclude.

The problem is that Thomasina's and Valentine's enthusiasm about a new world paradigm is not shared by others in the play. Lady Croom's general disapproval is an initial sign. Her mind is configured to accept the regularities of Newtonian order, and so are the minds of others. Reading Thomasina's essay on heat death, even her tutor Septimus responds, "You should not have written it . . . It will make me mad as you promised" (92). Even the iconoclastic tutor initially resists Thomasina's evidence.

That even twentieth-century minds have Newtonian configurations is verified by the separate endeavors of Hannah and Bernard, inhabitants of the play's contemporary set. Hannah uses her mind to try to prove that Sidley Park is paradigmatic of the nineteenth-century "decline from thinking to feeling" (27). She plans to use orderly thought to prove itself superior to the chaos/picturesque/romantic model, which she describes as the irregularity of sentiment. And Bernard's enterprise is to prove that Lord Byron was involved in a deadly 1809 duel at Sidley Park which would solve the mystery of his self-imposed exile thus far unexplained by scholars. In both cases, but especially for Bernard, evidence reveals itself not in a regular and linear fashion, but much as the leaf reveals itself on the algorithmic graph – unpredictable dot by unpredictable dot – to reveal a reality that evades predictability. Bernard proceeds linearly to his ultimate academic embarrassment, jumping to linearly logical conclusions rather than waiting for all the dots to reveal themselves. Likewise, Hannah's premises lead her to conclude that a minor nineteenth-century author deserves acclaim because of that author's craftlike sense of order, as opposed to the irregular and far more creative "ramblings" of her more famous contemporaries. In the process of individual awakening, Hannah learns the value of "feeling," and Bernard learns that a "logical" reconstruction of the past overlooks unforeseen trackings on his graph of historical reconstruction. They both learn something of the value of chaos, of the truth that unexpected order rises out of moments of uncertainty and disorder.

Utilizing these discussions of chaos and order, Stoppard focuses on the confused humanity of his characters, the fact that they are *not* in control of their lives as they publicly try to verify. Chloë, a twentieth-century girl pondering the nature of universal determinism and seemingly out of her realm as she pursues the thought, makes perhaps the most telling observation of all, a simple mind amidst posturing intellectuals: "The universe is deterministic all right, just like Newton said, I mean it's trying to be, but the only thing wrong is people fancying people who aren't supposed to be in that part of the plan" (73). Valentine puts it in more formal terms: "Ah, the attraction that Newton left out. All the way back to the apple in the garden" (74). If Chloë is right, human emotions are the "strange attractor" in human dynamics, the deterministically unpredictable side of humanity that confirms we are part of nature rather than its masters.

Stoppard takes this very human observation in *Arcadia* and generates perhaps the most poignant scene of his theatre thus far. Thomasina, on the eve of her sixteenth birthday, attempts to seduce her tutor, who uncharacteristically but honorably resists this young woman's advances. He does dance with her, and they fold into an onstage dance that includes characters from the twentieth century – not unlike the blending of jam and pudding. This waltz of the two worlds blends together in a scene of unstated eloquence, as the audience has been given information that on this night Thomasina will die in a house fire, leaving Septimus bereft and the twentieth-century investigators touched by what they discover. For all the intellectual argumentation that unfolds in the play, this touching, emotional scene reveals the power of "people fancying people" who are not supposed to be part of the plan, affirming the point that passion generates a deterministic unpredictability very much in line with the vision of chaos theory.

Stoppard's vision lies somewhere between the order and restraint of linear rationalism and the disorderly randomness of unbounded turmoil, somewhere between the either/or options typically placed before us. What he presents is a landscape of interacting order and disorder eternally and creatively at play. Ultimately, in *Arcadia* we have a fractal play demonstrating orderly disorder at work and reflecting chaotics existence at every scale.

Chapter 6

Love is in the air

> There was a wager ... as to whether a play can show the very truth
> and nature of love. I think you lost it today.
>
> *Shakespeare in Love* (148)

This chapter includes four works – *The Real Thing, Indian Ink, Shakespeare in Love*, and *The Invention of Love* – that focus on the nature of love. But as may be expected from a playwright whose works typically engage multiple topics simultaneously, love surfaces in numerous Stoppard plays not included in this section, *Jumpers, Night and Day, Arcadia, The Coast of Utopia*, and *Rock'n'Roll* certainly included. In fact, though Stoppard has often been condemned for being a too coldly analytical playwright, many of his works include genuine moments of emotional poignancy. Such moments, however, have been generally overshadowed by Stoppard's intellectual and farcical intensity. It was not really until the production of *The Real Thing* in 1982 that the general perspective on Stoppard began to shift and critics began to see levels of emotional honesty even in early works like *Rosencrantz and Guildenstern are Dead* and *Jumpers*. Directors likewise began creating revivals that tapped into emotions which had until then been downplayed in favor of the plays' many other Stoppardian strengths. So while this section looks at Stoppard and love as presented by *The Real Thing* and three successors, it is worth keeping in mind similar emotional dimensions in his many other works.

Conversely, insofar as it is true that his many other plays entwine love in their plots, it must be noted that his love stories are also far more than their billing might suggest. The following are works that remind us of Stoppard's interest in affairs of the heart, though even as he pursues such affairs, his plays entangle themselves with matters at first glance having little or nothing to do with love.

The Real Thing: what is really real?

> Exclusive rights isn't love, it's colonization.   *The Real Thing* (75)

A play in the realist tradition about a playwright going through the emotional turmoil of marital infidelity, *The Real Thing* (1982) has what many critics have called the intimate feel of autobiography. Stoppard is willing to agree that "a lot of it is auto something. Henry sounds off on the subject of writing in exactly the same way the reporters in *Night and Day* said exactly what I wanted to say about journalism."[1] Anthony Jenkins, on the other hand, appropriately qualifies this near confession: "*The Real Thing* may be his most direct confessional but it is also a hall of mirrors."[2] The nature of love is one central focus, but Stoppard's pursuit of the concept of authenticity – the "real thing" – takes him to places he has already visited, including the nature of art and of truth itself. What is the real thing is, as Jenkins notes, a hall of mirrors that intrigues Stoppard and finds a place in the affairs of love as in most things human. So even if there are autobiographical trails to follow in this play, other matters tantalize far more in the final analysis.

The Real Thing opens with a man confronting his wife about an affair he is certain she is having:

> MAX Are you going to tell me who it is?
> CHARLOTTE Who what is?
> MAX Your lover, lover.
> CHARLOTTE Which lover?
> MAX I assumed there'd only be the one.
> CHARLOTTE Did you?
> MAX Well, do you see them separately or both together? Sorry, that's not fair.   (14)

It is vintage Stoppard, crisp and seamless, familiar but without cliché. However, it does not sound quite "authentic" or realistic. It is a little too witty, polished, and controlled. It feels almost as if Stoppard is confirming the critical response that he is unable to write true emotions into his plays.

As the play's second scene begins, we realize we have been tricked. The first scene turns out to be a rehearsal of a play – *House of Cards* – written by Henry, who is married to the actress Charlotte and friend to the actor Max. Shortly, Stoppard will give us a scene of actual betrayal where Max is a real cuckold who melts into blithering wordlessness, an exhibition, presumably, of how people really behave when their lives come crumbling down. Unlike the banter of the first scene, the exchange reduces to halting inanities:

M A X You're filthy.
    You filthy cow.
    You rotten filthy –
    . . .
    It's not true is it?
A N N I E Yes.
M A X Oh, God.
    (*He stands up.*)
    Why did you?
A N N I E I'm awfully sorry, Max –
M A X (*Interrupting, suddenly pulled together*) All right. It happened. All
    right. It didn't mean anything.
A N N I E I'm awfully sorry Max, but I love him.
M A X Oh, no.
A N N I E Yes.
M A X Oh, no. You don't.   (35–36)

The confrontation does not happen with a stiff upper lip and witty quips reminiscent of a Noël Coward parlor play, but with emotions that have no linguistic
equivalents.

So we have the urbane first scene and the blithering subsequent scene, both
up for consideration as the real thing. Then we have the added conundrum of
considering which event constitutes the real thing as an artistic accomplishment, a matter complicated by the fact that authentic art is not the same as
authentic life. This is in turn complicated by the fact that we are in the theatre –
itself an illusionist house of cards – as we are trying to work through such
issues. It is the sort of situation that Stoppard relishes, being what Toby
Zinman calls "the problem of life and pleasure of the theatre."[3]

Following the Max and Annie confrontation, Annie points out to Henry that
she did not quite know how to behave with Max because she has never read
anything about how the *unrequiting* lover should behave: "Gallons of ink and miles
of typewriter ribbon expended on the misery of the unrequited lover; not a word
about the utter tedium of the unrequiting" (38). In a turn that hints at what
Stoppard will pursue in *The Invention of Love*, Annie implies that behavior is
conditioned by conventions formalized by art. Annie's words also recall the
Player's response in *Rosencrantz and Guildenstern are Dead*, when he speaks of
his own fabricated death as "the kind you do believe in, it's what's expected" (123).
How we behave and how we expect others to behave is not, strictly speaking,
"natural." What is real and what is not becomes increasingly difficult to distinguish.

Exactly how does art impact upon and influence human feelings? This
question is central to *The Real Thing* in ways not so evident in Stoppard's

earlier reflections on the nature of art. For one thing, the issues at hand have a personal flavor to them. Take the matter of taste, for example. Throughout a good deal of the play, Henry is preparing to go on the television show *Desert Island Discs*, where celebrity castaways list their favorite records. But here this intellectual, urbane playwright is forced to admit he likes lowbrow pop music like Neil Sedaka, Herman's Hermits, and the Supremes: "The Righteous Brothers' recording of 'You've Lost that Lovin' Feelin'' on the London label was possibly the most haunting, the most deeply moving noise ever produced by the human spirit" (24). Stoppard's most sophisticated character confesses this lowbrow taste in music, a taste that even seeing Maria Callas live could not alter. Taste is something of a mystery. And in this case it is a mystery Stoppard himself frequently experiences, himself being a pop music fan. How can it be explained? Is it art? Are the feelings it promotes authentic?

Simply calling taste a subjective matter is not enough for Stoppard. The case of Private Brodie, and the ensuing Justice for Brodie Committee that Annie heads, provide opportunity for extended conversation on the matter. Brodie is a soldier arrested for defacing public property during an anti-nuclear-weapons rally. Annie sees the arrest as an act of injustice perpetrated upon an idealistic and conscientious young man. Brodie wants to write a play defending himself, and Annie supports the project, asking Henry to help out. Henry refuses, and Annie complains that Henry is a snob who is jealous of Brodie's manuscript because Brodie is someone "who really has something to write about, something real" (50). She adds, "To you, he can't write. To him, write is all you *can* do" (50). At this point, Henry introduces what has become a famous Stoppardian declaration, that writing is like a cricket bat:

> This thing here which looks like a wooden club, is actually several pieces of particular wood cunningly put together in a certain way so that the whole thing is sprung, like a dance floor . . . If you get it right, the cricket ball will travel two hundred yards in four seconds, and all you've done is give it a knock like knocking the top off a bottle of stout, and it makes a noise like a trout taking a fly . . . What we're trying to do is write cricket bats, so that when we throw up an idea and give it a little knock, it might . . . *travel.* (51)

Good writing occurs in such a way that the craftsmanship is virtually undetectable and the effect is effortlessly stunning.

Brodie may or may not have an idea to throw up, but his writing is clearly not doing his idea a good service. Henry picks up Brodie's script and continues his thought:

7 *The Real Thing.* Directed by Peter Wood. Design: Carl Toms. Lighting: William Bundy. Roger Rees (Henry), Felicity Kendal (Annie). Strand Theatre, London, 1982

> Now, what we've got here is a lump of wood of roughly the same shape trying to be a cricket bat, and if you hit the ball with it, the ball will travel about ten feet and you will drop the bat and dance about shouting "Ouch!" with your hands stuck into your armpits. (*Indicating the cricket bat.*) This isn't better because someone says it's better . . . It's better because it's better.   (51)

Then Henry reads a bit of Brodie's manuscript aloud: "'You're a strange boy, Billy, how old are you?' 'Twenty, but I've lived more than you'll ever live.' Ooh, ouch!" (51). Thanks to the opening scene of *The Real Thing*, we know that Henry is capable of crafting a cricket bat of a scene. But is his work "real" and, if so, in what ways is it real?

The question of what is real in art and what is real in life continues toward play's end when Annie has an affair with a young co-actor while rehearsing, of all things, the seventeenth-century classic *'Tis Pity She's a Whore* (another mirror in this deepening hall). Discovering the infidelity, Henry's world begins to unravel when he meets up with his daughter and waxes philosophical, noting that everything is "about self-knowledge through pain" (61). Daughter Debbie responds, "No, it was about did she have it off or didn't she. As if having it off is infidelity" (61). She comfortably reduces sexuality to "biology" (62) and is convincing at least in her confidence, until dad calls it "persuasive nonsense. Sophistry in a phrase so neat you can't see the loose end that would unravel it. It's flawless but wrong" (62).

Henry further responds by offering a counterpoint to Debbie's free thinking: "Carnal knowledge. It's what lovers trust each other with. Knowledge of each other, not of the flesh but through the flesh, knowledge of self, the real him, the real her, in extremis, the mask slipped from the face" (62). But Debbie rivals Henry's skills with her own epigrammatic skills: "Exclusive rights isn't love, it's colonization" (63). We see here that skill can elevate unstable ideas to the level of apparent irrefutability, revealing once again that language is able to serve truth but also able to obfuscate and confuse.

Much is stripped bare, however, when Henry confronts Annie, who confesses her infidelity but implicates Henry by saying, "You have to find a part of yourself where I'm not important or you won't be worth loving" (71). Henry covers his hurt in a standard way, by suggesting a "dignified cuckoldry." But the witty façade doesn't hold up, and he finally admits, "I can't *find* a part of myself where you're not important" (75). Alternating between false bravado and helpless pleading, both characters dig for comfortable witticisms as they try to make their points. Through the stumbling, however, it becomes evident that love remains despite all reason for it to have been extinguished.

Henry and Annie are on the stage as the play draws to an end. Henry is on the phone congratulating Max who is announcing he is getting remarried, the result of one of those romantic "across the crowded room" encounters (81). Hearing that the bride is involved with theatre, Henry spouts one last witticism: "To marry one actress is unfortunate, to marry two is simply asking for it" (81). Finding a response by paraphrasing an Oscar Wilde epigram, Henry sounds suspiciously inauthentic when weighed against "real life" standards. But does it work as art? The question recalls Charlotte's own earlier epigrammatic observation: "the difference between plays and real life – thinking time" (21).

As Henry speaks on the phone, Annie turns off all the lights. Henry is distracted, sensing something in the air. Still on the phone, he clicks on the radio, and the Monkees' "I'm a Believer" fills the room. Still on the phone, Henry is anxious to get to Annie as the play ends with the Monkees song increasing in volume. The conclusion parallels the play's opening in general effect, using sound instead of sight to leave us wondering what is the real thing. Consider that throughout the play audiences are directed to be critical of Henry's lowly taste in music. Then, as the play ends, we are treated to a final scene that strives to touch us with that same music. What should we think? What should we feel? And is what we feel the real thing? Is it an "authentic" feeling, or is it mere manipulation? When a production succeeds at getting this ending to emotionally draw us in, the result is a lingering uncertainty about the nature of authentic art and authenticity in the real world.

What is the real thing? It is clearly and necessarily a many-layered thing which undermines exactly what a once confident Henry formerly believed. Moving from the aesthetic to the moral, we see similar uncertainties unfold. John Fleming says it best when he observes that for Henry – and apparently Stoppard, too – "a monogamous relationship is to be valued, respected, revered, and that monogamy is more meaningful and fulfilling than promiscuity, but Henry's moral order is flexible enough to view infidelity as understandable and forgivable."[4] Stoppard admits his own sentiments when he observes, "Morality aspires to a condition of being absolute (not relative) but culture seems more the product of social and aesthetic conditioning."[5] Art is at its best, it seems, when it recognizes absolutes but conditions us to embrace a spirit of flexibility, understanding, and forgiveness.

Indian Ink: never the twain . . .

> What a pity, though, that all his revolutionary spirit went into his life and none into his art.   *Indian Ink* (59)

Indian Ink (1995), a romantic face-off between East and West, is a reworking of Stoppard's radio play *In the Native State* (1991). The play is, as John Fleming notes, "tinged with sentiment, melancholy, nostalgia, and likeable characters."[6] Stoppard admits that it is "a very cosy play" with "no villains,"[7] drawing in part upon fond recollections of his time spent in India as a young child. However, Stoppard emphasizes that "the area in which I feed off myself is really much more to do with thoughts I have had rather than days I have lived."[8] Another former denizen of India, Felicity Kendal, contributed to the West End success of the play as Flora Crewes, a role seemingly custom-made for her.[9]

With the dexterity of its radio play origins, *Indian Ink* jumps from 1930 to several periods roughly equivalent to "today." It also geographically jumps between India and Britain. The effect is a lively exchange between past and present that pursues the question of historical recoverability, with a clash between East and West that challenges the notion that the two worlds are incommensurable. All of this is packed into an unlikely love story.

Flora – Stoppard's fictional poet and Bloomsbury literary celebrity – is an avid letter writer who sends everything to her younger sister, Eleanor. Much of the play is interspersed with Flora reading her letters aloud. They are telling commentary on the things Flora experiences during her brief 1930 stay in the native state of Jummapur. Signs of weakening British rule are beginning to show, with Indian nationalism revealing both its hope and dangers. We are given rumors of Gandhi and various rising protests, but this is all backdrop to what Stoppard does best, giving us two characters whose personal lives both anticipate and parallel the large sweeps of history that surround them.

Flora Crewes is a 35-year-old free-spirited poet out of the Bloomsbury tradition, who has escaped to India ostensibly for her health and who supports herself by lecturing on the London literary scene. Nirad Das, an Indian, meets Flora Crewes and instantly reveals himself to be an avid lover of everything English. He speaks the language impeccably, is widely read in English literature, and has even memorized the physical layout of a London he's never visited. As an artist he is captivated by pre-Raphaelite artists and all the European conventions of the time. The two instantly strike up a friendship, though it suffers from Nirad's pervading sense of subservience even as Flora insists that Das should show pride in his native culture and behave as an Indian national rather than as a British subject.

All of this pops up quickly in the play. Equally quickly we are introduced to Flora's aged younger sister Eleanor, alive today and holding onto her long-dead sister's letters and memorabilia. Scholar and biographer Eldon Pike persists in interviewing Eleanor in order to complete extensive footnotes to a collection of Crewes's letters that he will soon publish. His obsession with explanatory footnotes becomes something of a joke in the play; Stoppard has him frequently interrupt the action by inserting his footnoted – and often inaccurate – insights throughout the play.

About a year after this meeting with Pike, Eleanor receives a visit from Anish Das, the thoroughly English son of Nirad, who barely knew his father but recognized his "anonymous" portrait of Flora Crewes on the book cover of Pike's just-published *Collected Letters*. The two work to reconstruct the brief but influential relationship between their two relatives. As their reconstruction occurs, Nirad and Flora unfold their relationship onstage, and Pike, too, surfaces in India, trying himself to reconstruct the same relationship. Past and present never completely harmonize, though in many instances Stoppard has one or more of the reconstructions suggest answers to the unanswered questions of another reconstruction.

The play is another mystery piece for Stoppard, another study in the matter of recovering the past. We see a rising nationalist consciousness in Nirad, urged on by an anti-imperial sensibility on liberal-minded Flora's part. We see lingering prejudices slowly overcome on Eleanor's part along with an awakening desire to recover one's roots on Anish's part. Curiously, though, and true to Stoppard's point, not everything is revealed by play's end. We are still left wondering about the one truly sensational question of the play: did Flora sleep with Nirad or perhaps with someone else on that one fateful night that she cryptically writes about in a letter home to Eleanor? Fully recovering the past is finally impossible, as Stoppard has also noted in works from *Travesties* to *Arcadia*. But it is not something really to be worried about because the *spirit* of the past can be recovered even if the *factuality* of the past cannot. In this regard, Eleanor and Anish succeed where Pike does not. And Stoppard succeeds above all with *Indian Ink* itself.

Another attempt to capture the past surfaces in the play in the form of *Up the Country*, an 1866 travelogue by Emily Eden, an actual Victorian woman who was given the grand tour of India at the peak of its British transformation. Eden is not entirely comfortable with Britain's presence in India, cloaked as it is in Christian charity even as it displays racism, bigotry, and oppression at every greed-feeding turn. Das has a copy and gives it to Flora, suggesting that Das is not as genuinely subservient as he initially appears. Eden even gets the final word in the play (in Flora's voice): "I sometimes wonder they do not cut all our heads off and say nothing more about it" (83).

Like Stoppard's other plays, much in *Indian Ink* depends on Stoppard's decision to honor all sides. Flora is a compelling example of what is great, bold, and seductive about European culture. And Nirad is an equally seductive representative of his own culture. Things do not start off so well between the two, however, with Flora being overly sanctimonious and Nirad being too subserviently "Indian." After showing his groupie's knowledge of all things British, Nirad slips into an unsettling brown-face routine: "Oh, Miss Crewe, I am transported beyond my most fantastical hopes of our fellowship! This is a red-letter day without dispute!" (12). After a botched exchange where Flora tells him to be "less Indian," Flora finally says, "what I meant was for you to be *more* Indian, or at any rate *Indian*, not Englished-up and all over me like a Labrador" (12). Even the fact that they share the same language seems to be of little help: in one scene Das is in Flora's bedroom and asks to be able to sit closer to the door. Mildly annoyed at what seems to be unnecessary modesty, Flora says he can move onto the verandah for all she cares. Das actually just wants to sit by the door so he can smoke: "oh, I'm sorry" (43). It all fits into the multi-varied theme of misunderstanding between sexes, and among races and nations.

These multiple issues never surface so well as when Nirad offers to do a portrait of Flora, and the portrait disappointingly turns out to be in the tradition of European portraiture. Insisting that Das should not love all things English just because they are English, Flora asks: "Can't you paint me without thinking of Rossetti or Millais?" (44). Flora's well-intended liberalism leads her to try to convert Das into the sort of Indian *she* thinks Indians should be. Das, however, surprises all by being his own man: "I like the Pre-Raphaelites because they tell stories. That is my tradition, too. I am Rajasthani. Our art is narrative art, stories from the legends and romances" (45). He traces Indian tradition back farther than Shakespeare or Chaucer, which humbles Flora.

The perfectly proper son, Anish is himself an artist with an inclination toward contemporary European non-representationalism. He comes to learn the value of his native roots as he and Eleanor get closer to understanding the friendship between Nirad and Flora. He eventually concedes that this Indian obsession with all things English has been "a disaster for us. Fifty years of Independence and we are still hypnotized" (59).

A different portrait of Flora by Das, one that Anish and Eleanor have before them, offers an even more unique interplay between East and West. The woman, nude, is painted with standard European perspective, but the rest of the painting is flat and enamel, following Indian convention. Anish sees symbolism in the painting's house-within-a-house structure, but Eleanor only sees a room with a mosquito net surrounding a bed. Anish sees a book on a pillow as meaningful. Eleanor just says, "That's Flora" (68). Anish sees a vine with falling leaves as evidence that "my father knew your sister was dying." Eleanor says, "sometimes a vine is only a vine" (68). Looking at the same painting, the two see completely different realities, with the Eastern sensibility in this case revealing greater perception. And so too goes Stoppard's point about the world at large. Products of two cultures, Eleanor and Anish, Flora and Nirad, and even Pike and Dilip (Pike's Indian guide) use the same equipment – eyes, ears, etc. – and look out upon the same world, but what they see is not the same. But Stoppard makes this point of difference in general only to ingeniously undermine it in the particular, specifically in the realm of the heart.

Halfway through the play Das introduces the concept of *rasa*, which he describes as "what you must feel when you see a painting, or hear music; it is the emotion which the artist must arouse in you" (29). Das adds for Flora's benefit, "Poetry is a sentence whose soul is *rasa*" (29). Mere facts, mere history, lack *rasa*. The various portraits of Flora possess *rasa*, inspiring moments of keen emotional awareness. Flora's poetry, collected in *Indian Ink*

8 *Indian Ink*. Directed by Peter Wood. Design: Carl Toms. Lighting: Mark Henderson. Felicity Kendal (Flora Crewe), Art Malik (Nirad Das). Aldwych Theatre, London, 1995

and recited at various points throughout the play (they are Stoppard's own creations), is designed to inspire the same. Hopelessly separated at one level by gender, race, and culture, it is their intuitive understanding of this universal concept of *rasa* that brings these two souls together. The artist's enterprise is the instrument of union. Or so claims *Indian Ink*, itself an attempt to capture *rasa* on the stage.

At many levels the idea that East is East and West is West (and never the twain shall meet) is irrefutable. But at those intuitive levels that precede logic, thought, and language – at those odd points where art (like love) creates a bridge – then East and West (and any number of other apparent opposites) can sidestep the logical minds of prying rationalists like Eldon Pike and find places where the twain actually do meet.

Shakespeare in Love: a signature collaboration

> Strangely enough it all turns out well.   *Shakespeare in Love* (23)

Strange as it is to imagine, *Shakespeare in Love* would never have happened if it were not for Marc Norman, Stoppard's co-writer and the originator of the initial script. It is strange to imagine because this screenplay is so quintessentially "Stoppardian." Then again, given Stoppard's tendency to adapt other people's work into plays and movies, it may in fact be appropriate that Stoppard's strongest work in film is indebted to someone else for its inception.[10]

Shakespeare in Love gives flesh and blood to the revered corpse of the Bard, standardly imaged as perpetually middle-aged, staid, and respectable. What must the man have been like in the blush of youth and prime of life? There is plenty of historical evidence that Shakespeare was a lively, entertaining companion, quick-witted, generous, and roguishly impetuous. *Shakespeare in Love* captures what Stoppard and Norman imagine to be the vitality of a man so immensely capable of observing and reporting the heart of human nature.

We first see Will scribbling multiple versions of his signature,[11] an indication that he is really not terribly sure who he is. We learn fairly quickly that he has already written several plays, though they seem to be poor imitations of Kit (Christopher) Marlowe's sensational new theatre. And he suffers from writer's block, having lost his muse, "fair Rosaline," who turns out to be little more than an opportunistic theatre groupie. Prospects are bleak.

Then there is the foolhardiness of trying to make a living in the theatre in general. A good deal of the humor stems from a point made by Marc Norman, a film industry veteran: "The Elizabethans were inventing our business."[12] The point inspires numerous comically anachronistic inserts, like an analyst who comes complete with business couch, a good-hearted but dim-witted theatre owner (Henslowe), and a loanshark turned producer who becomes a theatre convert (Fennyman). Strangely enough, the business has much the same magical allure then that it has even now, despite Henslowe's summary of the situation: "The natural condition is one of insurmountable obstacles on the road to imminent disaster. Believe me, to be closed by the plague is a bagatelle in the ups and downs of owning a theatre." Fennyman asks, "So what do we do?" to which Henslowe replies, "Nothing. Strangely enough it all turns out well." "How?" asks Fennyman. "I don't know. It's a mystery" (23). Then, as if on cue, a Messenger arrives: "The theatres are reopened," guaranteeing at least a hope of all things turning out well.

When the play they are mounting is actually put on, and when all the wheels seem to be falling off, Will moans, "We are lost." Henslowe, ever the optimist, responds "No, it will turn out well." "How will it?" "I don't know. It's a mystery" (131–32). The lines are repeated moments later when it is discovered that the boy playing Juliet has lost his girlish voice. How will the show go on? "I don't know. It's a mystery" (135). And then, toward the end, when Viola transforms her personal misfortunes into a plot that will become Will's next play, she says that all will end well, to which a skeptical Will asks, "How does it?" Rather than Henslowe, it is Viola, Will's muse and undying love, who speaks: "I don't know. It's a mystery" (152). And it does end well, at least in art, poetry, the imagination. If it is impossible in real life for a lady to marry a "Bankside poet and player" (66), there are still the fruits of pleasures past to savor in the imagination and in the ever-present art it generates. Instead of seeing "a watery end" to their love, imagination and art can generate "a new life beginning on a stranger shore" (154). For Viola, it is the literal new shore of Virginia with her new and unloving husband, but that shore will be filled with the memory of true love hardly experienced even by the greatest majesties of the land. For Will, his stranger shore will remain the theatre, reinvigorated as he is by his love for the lost Viola. The film moves Shakespeare from trying to write the fantastical *Romeo and Ethel the Pirate's Daughter* to a production of *Romeo and Juliet* that captures the essence of the love and life he experiences with Viola. And from there, he matures into a man who can capture his broken heart in the soon-to-be *Twelfth Night*.

Romeo and Ethel the Pirate's Daughter is swashbuckling melodrama of the lowest order. Henslowe, "the businessman with a cash flow problem" (1), wants a romantic comedy full of action, including a show-stopping scene with a dog – all the rage even at Elizabeth's court. Henslowe calls the play "a crowd tickler – mistaken identities, a shipwreck, a pirate king, a bit with a dog, and love triumphant" (3). The comic resolution will come about when the plot reveals "Romeo to be the very same Capulet cousin stolen from the cradle and fostered to manhood by his Montague mother that was robbed of her own child by the Pirate king" (39). This farcical plot, sounding something like Wilde's *The Importance of Being Earnest*, is the wistful stuff that may sustain an entertainment industry, but it comes nowhere close to the life-enhancing art that Will seeks and that *Shakespeare in Love* becomes.

Curiously enough, *Shakespeare in Love* begins with a title card seemingly announcing a play entitled "THE LAMENTABLE TRAGEDIE OF THE MONEY-LENDER REVENG'D" (1). It actually turns out to be the title card for the film proper, a tale of Henslowe's cashflow problems and Fennyman the money-lender's effort at recovery. This slippage between film and play reflects the slippage between disorderly life and orderly art that persists throughout the movie.

We see love in "real" life unfold as the movie progresses, leaving Will speechless in its presence. When Will and Viola first meet at a dance – in something of the fashion in which Romeo will meet Juliet – Viola asks of the speechless

Will, "I heard you are a poet … But a poet of no words?" (44). Shaken out of his silence too late to respond to Viola (reminding us of *The Real Thing*: "the difference between plays and real life – thinking time," 21), he finally finds the mistimed words to tell a senseless, uncaring Wessex, "I was a poet till now, but I have seen beauty that puts my poems at one with the talking ravens at the Tower" (44).

Art requires grounding in the real for it to be more than the poor shadows Will has thus far created. On a very minor but fairly comical level, we see art draw from reality when the ranting Puritan Makepeace, crying out against the two playhouses in town, bellows, "I say a plague on both their houses" (8), clearly within earshot of Will the linguistic pack rat. And he borrows the famous balcony scene from his own first private encounter with Viola. The favor is returned by art to real life when Will takes an innocent speech from his play and adds a bawdy touch by telling Viola, in bed: "Stay but a little, I will come again" (83). But these mere trifles are nothing compared to the larger matters at play. Mastery of the world through art or at least through artifice is Will's special talent, and his particular skill is language: "for sixpence a line I could cause a riot in a nunnery" (9). But without inspiration he is all prose and no poetry. Rosaline turns out to be no inspiration, unless Will perhaps chooses to continue down the *Pirate King* trail. Kit Marlowe offers advice to a reluctantly receptive Will, putting him on track to write the character Mercutio. But it is Will's romantic entanglement with the passionate and equally romantic Viola De Lesseps that puts him on the scent of passion and art.

When we meet the woman who will change Will's life, she is herself little more than an overly romantic dreamer who insists, "I will have poetry in my life. And adventure. And love. Love above all" (21). Viola does not know where to find love, except perhaps in the theatre, but she is smart enough to long for "not the artful postures, but love that overthrows life" (21). When she finally meets Will, the poet whose work she admires from afar, the intrigued woman mildly despairs that it is the tongue-tied man at the ball. What has captured her heart at this point is not the man but the man's poetry.

Up to now art has only glancingly expressed the full measure of real-life love, if we are to believe Queen Elizabeth, the period's famous "virgin" queen. She argues that to this point she has seen "playwrights teach nothing about love, they make it pretty, they make it comical, or they make it lust. They cannot make it true" (94). This comes from a woman who sacrificed love in the name of duty to god and country. Indeed, "duty" seems to be the one thing Will knows little about, having left his wife and family in Stratford and having played the two theatre groups off against each other without any sign of loyalty to one or the other. His only apparent loyalty is to "love," which "knows nothing of rank or riverbank. It will spark between a queen and the poor vagabond who plays the king, and their love should be minded by each, for love denied blights the soul we owe to God" (66). Romantic stuff of idle dreamers and inexperienced Romeos destined to suffer the pains of forbidden love. The real world does know something of rank and riverbank, a fact that Will's romanticism must come to terms with, even as Viola learns that her duty is to her parents and to her sovereign, including entrance into a loveless marriage as a matter of duty. This the Queen already knows, and she accepts at this point that theatre is merely entertainment put on to while away the time. Viola disagrees, however, and, forgetting herself, interrupts the Queen to say she believes there is one playwright who can bring truth to the stage. Through several curious twists, a wager is made between Will and Lord Wessex, witnessed by the Queen. It will be paid when a play is written that can "show us the very truth and nature of love" (95).

Increasingly, the difference between rehearsals and real life blurs. The rehearsed melee between Montagues and Capulets transforms into a real donnybrook between Henslowe's troupe and the Chamberlain's Men, so confusing that an uncomprehending Fennyman critically exclaims, "Wonderful, wonderful! And a dog!" (100). More notably for Will and Viola, scenes of rehearsal converge with events beyond the stage, and the near ecstasy of the art/reality conflation provides a brief period of pleasure they will likely never experience again. Too soon the harsh edges of reality cut into the dream world they have created. Viola hears that Will is married, and everyone hears of Marlowe's death. In an instant, Will loses his love and feels overwhelming guilt that he has caused Marlowe's death. When Viola mistakenly thinks the general mourning is over the death of Will rather than Marlowe, her own grief sinks to great depths as well.

When the two are finally reunited, circumstances have made being together impossible. Love and pain flow together. And Will knows that desire cannot overcome duty. He, like his Romeo, is "fortune's fool" who at best can grasp at fleeting moments of felicity. Viola must be wed, and she must leave for the shores of her husband's Virginia plantations.[13]

But before grim reality settles into the business of doing its duty, there is what art can do. *Romeo and Juliet* effectively bottles the lightning passion and pain of Will and Viola, immortalizing their brief encounter on life's stage. A now married Viola escapes her husband, runs to the theatre one last time, and dons the garb of Juliet opposite Will's Romeo in order to save the performance. Their own real-world love entangles with the passions of the play, once again to the point that play and reality become indistinguishable. Even Fennyman is transformed by what he witnesses. Even the Puritan Makepeace – swept into the theatre against his will – exultantly throws kisses onto the stage.

And even Elizabeth, decades past her own moments of passionate entanglement, sees that Wessex has lost his wager "as to whether a play can show the very truth and nature of love" (148). When the crestfallen Wessex asks, not about the play, but about his life in general, "How is this to end?" (149), Elizabeth responds – without appealing to mystery – "As stories must when love's denied – with tears and a journey. Those whom God has joined in marriage, not even I can put asunder" (150). Unlike the stage, real life offers no last-minute reprieve. No pirate king to the rescue. No apothecary's tricks. Life moves forward against human desire and in fulfillment of inescapable duty.

But art gives us the opportunity to relive these moments of ecstasy, though admittedly at one remove. Art can kindle momentary joy amid the ashes of living despair. That is what we see as Elizabeth takes control of events and crafts her own little world of illusion by pretending not to recognize Viola dressed as a boy actor. She insists Viola *is* a boy actor, saving the day and the illusion, and preserving the moment for Viola and Will. Reclaiming joy through art is what Will and Viola fabricate slightly later as they spend their last moments together outlining a play about forlorn love salvaged on a foreign shore. Capturing what they have just experienced on the stage and in their lives, Viola warns of the Viola that will become the character in *Twelfth Night*, "Be fearful of her virtue, she comes ... dressed as a boy" (152).

Love lasts not in life but in its artistic distillation. Art enriches life even as life's experiences enrich art. But if this interdependent circle makes sense, so does another way to look at it all. Art is a part of life, giving us dreamy hope that someday we will once again reach that far shore where everything, though only fleetingly, comes together in perfect harmony. But if it does not come together again, art is there to provide the distant echo of the music that once was.

The Invention of Love: Victoriana made curious

> He is spoiled, vindictive, utterly selfish and not very talented. But these
> are merely the facts.   *The Invention of Love* (95)

There is hardly any way to describe *The Invention of Love* (1997) without making it sound pretty uninteresting to the general public. It is about a Cambridge don, A. E. Housman (1859–1936), who was an obsessively precise classicist and a minor poet whose unrequited homosexual passion left him resigned to a life of esoteric scholarship and mournful poetry. The play opens in 1936 with the dead AEH crossing the River Styx. The ferryman, Charon, waits for a scholar and a poet, only to be surprised that the description applies to one man and not two. Though the play does split AEH in two, it is by age rather than occupation, with a young Housman entering the scene and defending his life against the deceased AEH. Other literary notables appear, including John Ruskin, Walter Pater, and Benjamin Jowett. Oscar Wilde also enters the play, though not as the urbane wit of his youth but as the broken man who has been humiliated and imprisoned for crimes against nature.

While *The Invention of Love* does not have the comic flair of most of Stoppard's previous work, it does have its moments and is distinctly Stoppardian in other regards.[14] The play is AEH's recollection of life, recalling Stoppard's use of the filtering character Henry Carr in *Travesties*. And Stoppard returns once again to the literal doubling of his central character. Stoppard notes about his twinning interest, "I could write an awfully good book about The Plays of Tom Stoppard – to me, it's so obvious: many of my plays are about unidentical twins, about double acts. Twins in *Hapgood*; the two Housmans here."[15] And he reveals that his interest in Housman involved the man's "Romantic/ classicist contrast," adding "It's *Arcadia* again."[16] The play is a return to Stoppard's sense that humanity is torn between these two opposing outlooks toward life.

The Invention of Love opens with expected Stoppardian flair as AEH, deceased classics scholar, meets Charon, the mythological guardian of the entrance to Hades. Offstage barking promises a meeting with the three-headed dog Cerberus just ahead. But rowing into view are three men in a boat and a yapping dog (recalling Stoppard's adaptation of *Three Men in a Boat*, actually referred to toward the end of the play [101]), all enjoying a summer afternoon in the Oxfordshire countryside. One of the men is the young college student Housman; the others are friends, and they are all very much alive. AEH watches in amazement as he sees his former self and his once and only love interest, Moses Jackson, innocently banter back and forth. AEH has nothing but his past to look forward to as Charon rows him off into the mist. Stoppard gives us a pretty intriguing opening, once again.

Housman's attraction to the young athlete Jackson is immediate, though Jackson sees only friendship unfolding between the two men. Housman uses his brilliant classical background to drop subtle hints: "To a Roman, to call something *Greek* meant – very often – sissylike, or effeminate. In fact, a hoop, a *trochos*, was a favourite gift given by a Greek man to the boy he, you know, to his favourite boy" (7). Housman discovers pretty quickly that the kindly but conventional Jackson is far more the Roman warrior than the Greek lover, but

9 *The Invention of Love*. Directed by Richard Eyre. In a punt: (rear)
Michael Bryant (Charon), (front) John Wood (AEH). National
Theatre/Cottesloe Theatre, 1997

Housman persists, following Jackson into a patent office clerkship and even
pursuing him when Jackson announces his betrothal and impending marriage.

But *The Invention of Love* is not some salacious tale of forbidden love.
Stoppard uses his many Oxford-trained characters to present a far more interesting – though definitely less sensational – play about the nature of love that we
all so heartily take for granted as always having been what it is today.

The play is set within the elite intellectual surroundings of Oxford University,
where Victorian propriety is properly codified and manifest. Benjamin Jowett,
John Ruskin, and Walter Pater are the play's old guard, debating issues of beauty

and morality and looking for an ideal to hold up for contemporay emulation. Jowett argues, "Nowhere was the ideal of morality, art, and social order realized more harmoniously than in Greece in the age of the great philosophers" (17). But in order to celebrate the glory of Greece, they concede they would have to ignore the infamous Greek "buggery" that was so central to the era. Pater turns to late fifteenth-century Italy as his ideal, but then concedes that morality and social order were not particular Italian strengths. Ruskin argues in favor of the medieval Gothic period, insisting to everyone's grudging concession that "medieval Gothic cathedrals ... were the great engines of art, morality, and social order" (17). But then the period also fired intense intolerance. None of their arguments withstands scrutiny, suggesting that finding precedent for an ideal code of human behavior is impossible.

When the students take the stage, they discuss the celebrated love of Catullus and Lesbia. Jackson asks the traditionalist question, "Did they get married?" to which Pollard (with Housman's support) explains: "No. They loved, and quarreled, and made up, and loved, and fought, and were true to each other and untrue. She made him the happiest man in the whole world and the most wretched, and after a few years she dies, and then, when he was thirty, he died, too" (13). Love is a dash of emotions that follows its own inscrutable logic. That is nothing new, of course. But what Pollard says next *is* something new: although Catullus dies, his love persists, because "by that time Catullus had invented the love poem" (13). The word "invented" is central, as Pollard makes clear: "Like everything else, like clocks and trousers and algebra, the love poem had to be invented." He continues: "After millenniums of sex and centuries of poetry ... *that* was invented in Rome in the first century before Christ" (13).

Stoppard's point relating to love parallels much of what he says in general about the human urge to classify and categorize: love is inexplicable until conventions are introduced that help to describe what it is. That is the positive side of the enterprise. The problem arises when the conventions of description legislatively restrict growth, change, or evolution. In the case of love, once it becomes conventionalized – as in the case of courtly romance, for example – then it loses freedom to pursue its own natural course.

Amid this institutionalizing bluster comes mention of Oxford's most brilliant student, Oscar Wilde, iconoclast of the first order and evidence that defining proper human behavior can have life-strangling consequences. Going beyond the academic debates of these scholars, the play introduces Henry Labouchere (played by the same actor who plays Ruskin), the MP whose 1885 "gross indecency" legislation outlawed homosexual behavior in England. Legislated morality, love defined, finds its way into late Victorian culture, and it is the law that famously entangles and imprisons Oscar Wilde.

Focusing on forbidden homosexual passions works for Stoppard as the perfect topic for how love suffers under social sanction. Even though such practices have occurred for millennia even among the most civilized of cultures, Victorian mandate (and similar mandates by other eras as well) defines homosexual love as "unnatural" and thereby works to prevent love from running this particular course. Love has been defined to exclude homosexuality. Against this point, Stoppard rather ingeniously draws upon an actual (or at least mythical) precedent of the full force of love without restriction when he has Housman report an account of

> an army, a hundred and fifty pairs of lovers, the Sacred Band of Theban youths, and they were never beaten till Greek liberty died for good at the battle of Chaeronea. At the end of that day, says Plutarch, the victorious Philip of Macedon went forth to view the slain, and when he came to the place where the entire three hundred fought and lay dead together, he wondered, and understanding that it was the band of lovers, he shed tears and said, whoever suspects baseness in anything these men did, let him perish.   (43)

Clearly, love can be a transforming force possessed of and generated by a logic of its own, capable of inspiring great sacrifice and unifying strength. Is this love any less true than the love between Catullus and Lesbia?

Pater is among the old guard that argues against rigid specifications: "The Renaissance teaches us that the book of knowledge is not to be learned by rote but is to be written anew in the ecstasy of living each moment for the moment's sake" (19). Against his peers his arguments fail to convince. Others, however, not only accept such words but live by them, Oscar Wilde certainly being the main example.

Rejected by Jackson, Housman ultimately turns to another "passion," a pursuit of scholarship. At first glance Housman's scholarly dedication seems to be a withdrawal from a life of disappointment. But Housman becomes a successful classical scholar. And in a manner somewhat reminiscent of Catullus himself, he overcomes the disappointments of love by generating poetry of love unrequited. Housman's poetry collection *A Shropshire Lad* is a lugubrious work that touches upon the kind of liking "better than suits a man to say" (89). Poet, scholar, celebrated Cambridge don, Housman's life is complete if not as passionate or sensational as that of his fellow collegian Oscar Wilde, though in its way, Housman's life of quiet determination succeeds where Wilde's sensational burnout at the hands of a moralistic judiciary almost certainly fails. From this point of view the play is a demonstration of the limitations of life in the face of the dream world of art. And as the play unfolds, there is a rising sense that such is

10 *The Invention of Love*. Directed by Jack O'Brien. Left to right: Robert Sean Leonard (Housman), Richard Easton (AEH). Vivian Beaumont Theater at Lincoln Center, 2001

the life of most human beings. If this were all, then *The Invention of Love* would have better been *The Invention of Regret*.

But there is another view that stands alongside this one. Stoppard allows Wilde the opportunity to point out: "The betrayal of one's friends is a bagatelle in the stakes of love, but the betrayal of oneself is a lifelong regret" (95). Wilde insists he has no regrets in his life despite having fallen from public grace and having been imprisoned for his homosexuality. The lack of regret is not the result of some "better to have loved and lost" cliché. Rather it is because of what became of the material of his life. Wilde admits that Bosie was "spoiled, vindictive, utterly selfish, and not very talented," but he adds that "these are merely the facts" (95). To Wilde, "The truth is he was Hyacinth when Apollo loved him . . . from his red rose-leaf lips comes music that fills me with joy" (95). The truth is that love roosted in Wilde's breast as a result of his love of even this most imperfect human being because "before Plato could describe love, the loved one had to be invented. We could never love anybody if we could see past our invention" (95). For Wilde, "Bosie is my creation, my poem" (95). If anything, Wilde's consummate success was seeing through his humiliation and recalling the beauty that was his highly imaginative life.

And so too for Housman. Even though his own love, Jackson, was a bit dense, unimaginative, and dull, to Housman, Jackson was *his* Hyacinth when

Apollo loved him. Housman observes, "When thou art kind I spend the day like a god; when thy face is turned aside, it is very dark with me" (102). In the end Housman, too, sees the beauty of his own less celebrated life, ending the play (as AEH) saying "how lucky to find myself standing on this empty shore, with the indifferent waters at my feet" (102).

Invention and attendant definition are necessary for all things, even the most natural-seeming of phenomena. Otherwise formlessness prevails. The key here is that invention of something as intensely personal as love requires broadly sanctioned parameters capable of embracing the widest possible range of individual inventions. Even love "better than suits a man to say" (89) should be permitted into the pantheon of types.

Chapter 7

Politics humanized

> Theories don't guarantee social justice, social justice tells you if a
> theory is any good.   *Squaring the Circle* (251)

As noted earlier, Stoppard rarely lobbies for or against particular political agendas in his theatre, repeatedly insisting that if you have a situation requiring immediate change, "you could hardly do worse than write a play about it." Rather, Stoppard's theatre is designed with the understanding that lasting change requires altered attitudes prior to – or simultaneous with – political legislation.

When Stoppard does address matters of a political nature in his plays, it is generally of a more abstracted nature, primarily involving institutionalized violations of individual human rights: "I don't lose any sleep if a policeman in Durham beats somebody up, because I know it's an exceptional case ... What worries me is not the bourgeois exception but the totalitarian norm."[1] This sentiment has led him on numerous occasions to write about the Soviet empire during its final years, resulting in such fine minor works as *Professional Foul* (1977), *Every Good Boy Deserves Favor* (1977), *Cahoot's Macbeth* (1979), and *Squaring the Circle, Poland 1980–81* (1984).

But though Stoppard targets the legacy of Eastern Bloc totalitarianism in these political critiques, he is not necessarily an apologist for Western democracies. In *The Dog It Was That Died, Neutral Ground,* and *Hapgood* Stoppard focuses on very conscientious characters in the politically ambiguous positions of being double or triple agents. Their dilemma of affiliation underscores Stoppard's point that it is immaterial which ideological side you are on if each side sacrifices the rights of the individual in the name of a given dogma. In *The Dog It Was That*

Died, Blair tries to remind Purvis why he should remain with the West. But Purvis stabs at Western vulnerabilities when he asks what freedom is if it "merely benefits the people who already have the edge?" (18). So, to the degree that Stoppard is political, he is most simply anti-totalitarian and anti-discriminatory, a not particularly unique or intriguing position to take.

What is intriguing, however, is how Stoppard looks at politics as something other than a stand-alone discipline. Key to Stoppard's position is the point that Henry makes in *The Real Thing*: "Public postures have the configuration of private derangement" (32–33). Stoppard's is a position that follows the Aristotelian observation that virtually all human activity is "political." Furthermore, Stoppard steadfastly believes that "all political acts have a moral basis to them and are meaningless without it."[2] Put quite simply, politics has its origins in the moral obsessions of those who capture the public imagination. This is the point (or one of the points) of Stoppard's portrayal of Lenin in *Travesties*. And it is found in *Rosencrantz and Guildenstern are Dead* as well: a dysfunctional family generates collateral damage that destroys a kingdom and all its hangers-on. The point arises in different guises throughout Stoppard's canon.

One of the "private derangements" that Stoppard persistently targets is less a political or theoretical position than it is a way of thinking. The target, loosely labeled "idealism," is a form of thinking that pursues something higher or better than is currently available. Generally speaking, idealism is considered a good thing, inspiring humanity to reach beyond its current grasp. But for Stoppard, it is the root of countless human disasters, great and small, brought on by dreamers who lose contact with the simple realities of life, destroying the present as they pursue a future that may never materialize. Culminating in *The Coast of Utopia*, Stoppard argues throughout that high-minded idealism invariably crumbles in the face of life and living, leaving pain and suffering in its wake.

In short, Stoppard's art takes on a political resonance by critiquing the thinking that leads to the misguided ideals that frequently take down whole worlds through their stubborn implementation. Life needs to ground itself in reality, and understanding the nature of that reality is humanity's most important task, without which only disaster can result.

The Coast of Utopia: the offshoring of politics

> When we have found all the mysteries and lost all the meaning, we will be alone, on an empty shore.   *Arcadia* (94)

The Coast of Utopia (2002) is a massive three-play project drawn from several very notable sources, including Isaiah Berlin's *Russian Thinkers* (1978) and

Shlomo Barer's *The Doctors of Revolution: 19th-Century Thinkers Who Changed the World* (2000). The resulting trilogy covers the broad span of nineteenth-century European history that eventually led to the momentous Russian Revolution of the early twentieth century. Every significant character in the play is drawn from actual historical figures. The three-play experience – whether seen in one day or viewed over a period of days – is much like reading a great Russian or Victorian novel.

The scope is truly impressive. But despite its scope, Jim Hunter is right when he observes that *The Coast of Utopia* "turns out also to be [Stoppard's] most domestic," given that the broad sweep of history both rises from and intertwines with the family lives of those involved. The result is what Hunter sees as a "decent humanism ... held up against murderous dogma."[3] Critic Ben Brantley makes a similar point by broadly observing that "intellectual history is forever being overwhelmed by the rush of the real."[4] What occurs is a continuation of a pattern that Stoppard has used throughout his career, wherein big ideas and rationalist-informed theories engage forces of real life, and real life wins out. *Arcadia* recruits chaos theory to make this point, encouraging us to live life in harmony with – not struggling against – patterns of the natural world. And it is a descriptive theory of existence that can be applied to *Coast* as well, full of self-similar recurrences and unpredictable causalities that we strive to manipulate at our own peril.

History for Stoppard is a series of repeated resemblances but never precise duplications, lacking the linear inevitability we like to believe it has. To highlight the pattern of recurrence and similarity that Stoppard sees, he rearranges chronology throughout the trilogy (using the same structural strategy he used in *Arcadia* and *The Invention of Love*), taking every opportunity to encourage us to make connections and draw conclusions in ways that extend beyond a simple sense of chronological linearity. Bounding through time and space to see parallels and unexpected influences, the result is a lesson in history demonstrating that searching for predictable outcomes is little more than a fool's errand. For example, Karl Marx surfaces throughout the play, but he is little more than an annoyance to those he encounters, making it virtually impossible to look at him and predict that the full sway of the butterfly effect would sweep this little man to the colossal status he reaches in the twentieth century.

Put another way, the play reveals that history repeatedly undermines the Hegelian insistence that it is dialectically inevitable, meandering instead on its own course without any regard for linear explicability. Inevitability only seems to occur when humanity attempts to channel the course of history, and it typically arrives in some form of catastrophe. Like Stoppard's inscrutable

Ginger Cat, history has its own logic, is impossible to anticipate, and is guaranteed to make a fool of anyone who tries to make it serve a particular end.

To date, the trilogy has been given two major productions. The 2002 London production directed by Trevor Nunn was summarized by many – to quote Jim Hunter – as "too long, too uneven, and too unrewardingly earnest, from a dramatist who until then had been reliably entertaining."[5] But as testament to the importance of a production that understands its script and benefits from its predecessor, Ben Brantley's review of the 2006 Lincoln Center opening of *Part One: Voyage* reports a far different result:

> The play may have been written by a man in his 60s, and its principal performers are at least into their 30s, yet even more than in its London incarnation at the National Theater, where I saw it four years ago, "Voyage" is paced and defined by the quicksilver changes of mood and conviction that come from being young in a time of flux – by the feeling that everything and nothing is possible. It's a work infused with the metabolism that lets college students talk furiously until dawn about big thoughts they are sure have never been thought before.[6]

The entire trilogy as staged by the Lincoln Center under the direction of Jack O'Brien was recognized for its fast-paced, highly theatrical staging. Ambitious and very thought-provoking, the work needs to be approached with the energy of youth: pausing and pondering the dense material may serve after-hours, but trying to put everything on centerstage for full speculation is simply an impractical goal. The point is one that is relevant to virtually all of Stoppard's plays, but is absolutely crucial for a play of this scope.

The trilogy follows a band of idealistic Russian intellectual revolutionaries initially swept away by the myriad treatises on freedom and equality generated throughout Germany and France. The long history that Stoppard plays out centrally includes the shipwreck of the 1848 French Revolution, a catastrophe generated by victims of oppression as much as by their oppressors. Though the spirit of revolution is kept alive and does lead to the Russian emancipation of the serfs in 1861, there is a pervading sense of failure generated by comparing rather modest accomplishments against initial utopian goals. The high ideals of complete justice and equity envisioned by these revolutionary idealists were far from achieved.

Part One: Voyage

> Man is where meaning begins to show.
> *The Coast of Utopia, Part One: Voyage* (17)

Voyage begins on the estate of Alexander Bakunin, patriarch of a family of four daughters and a son, educated in Europe (receiving a doctorate in philosophy from Padua), humanistic and progressive by inclination. But he is clearly an aristocrat, a major landowner and owner of hundreds of serfs (called "souls" by their owners). His daughters and wife possess European refinement and intellectual curiosity. Raised under the same liberal influences, Alexander's son, Michael, arrives onstage as a well-meaning, charismatic, but utterly irresponsible dreamer. Michael's circle of friends includes university students whose educations have made them dream with revolutionary fervor and put them onto careers of literary and journalistic pretension, lovers particularly of German idealism and French romanticism. Their desire above all else is to change the world, or, if not the world, at least Russia. What happens throughout the play – and this is important – is that Stoppard interweaves the personal travails of this family with the larger swaths of history by taking the grand ideas that are sweeping across the stage and showing them at work within this family.

The estate, Premukhino, is idyllic, an arcadian wonderland where high ideals can blossom in an agrarian dream world that exists only because of

11 *The Coast of Utopia: Voyage*. Directed by Jack O'Brien. Standing: Ethan Hawke (Michael Bakunin); left to right: Jennifer Ehle (Liubov Bakunin), Kellie Overbey (Tatiana Bakunin), Amy Irving (Varvara Bakunin). Vivian Beaumont Theater at Lincoln Center, 2006

the blood, sweat, and toil of the virtually invisible, long-suffering serfs. As long as they are invisible, all is well for these aristocratic dreamers. Alexander sets the tone early on: "All my daughters have been educated in five languages – call me liberal if you like. I read Rousseau as a young man, I was there at the storming of the Bastille, not storming it personally but I remember *my* feelings were decidedly mixed, that's how liberal I was when I was nineteen" (1). In this self-description, Alexander captures the essence of most of the Russian revolutionaries who populate *The Coast of Utopia*. They are decidedly interested in revolution, in real change; but the urge is for an orderly, rational, reasonable, and controlled revolution. And they oddly believe that they have the power to control the forces of change. Through the next generation of cataclysm, Alexander Bakunin will stand by these beliefs while others will not stand their ground quite so honorably.

Michael Bakunin, on the other hand, can best be described as a "force of nature." He deserts the army (and every other duty given him) as he discovers the liberating philosophy of romantic idealism. He intercedes in the matter of family matchmaking, arguing in the case of one sister, "To give oneself without love is a sin against the inner life. The outer world of material existence is mere illusion" (8). Michael uses his nearly operatic enthusiasm to infect his family with imported German idealism:

> Dawn has broken! In Germany the sun is already high in the sky! It's only us in poor behind-the-times Russia who are the last to learn about the great discovery of the age. The life of the Spirit is the only real life: our everyday existence stands between us and our transcendence to the Universal Idea where we become one with the absolute.   (7)

Michael enthuses over Kantian philosophy which insists that each individual should govern his own destiny by tapping into this "life of the Spirit." This initial imprint on Michael's consciousness will stay with him throughout his life and throughout the three plays, creating an unapologetic anarchist whose head stays up in the clouds and whose bold effervescence gives color to a dreamy idealism that is both attractive in its rejection of "duty" and unrealistic for more than one person at a time. After all, it takes family, servants, and resources of all sorts to support this Pan-like parasite whose ideas tantalize but also damage and destroy. Enthusiasm has its rewards but reality still needs to be tended to.

Michael joins a philosophical circle that studies Kant, Schiller, Fichte, Hegel, and other German thinkers, drawing his sisters into this community and generating intellectual enthusiasm verging on ecstasy. One of the crowd, Stankevich, points out, "The universe is all of a oneness, not just a lot of bits which happen to be lying around together . . . There is a meaning to it all, and Man is where the meaning begins to show" (17). Without humanity, the universe is meaningless. This empowering vision argues that humanity is actively enfolded into the world in a manner without which the world would not be. German idealism is indeed a mesmerizing philosophy.

The argument implicit in all this enthusiasm is that mankind must move beyond its eighteenth-century reliance on disaffected, objective reason. Another enthusiast, Belinsky, suggests that the "divine spark in man" is "some kind of intuition or vision, perhaps like the moment of inspiration experienced by the artists" (36). Belinsky argues long and hard about the virtues of artistic inspiration, a magical and inexplicable process that transcends rational explanation. He adds:

> When philosophers start talking like architects, get out while you can, chaos is coming. When they start laying down rules for beauty, blood in the streets is from that moment inevitable. When reason and measurement are made authorities for the perfect society, seek sanctuary among the cannibals.   (38)

The world, in short, needs to follow paths outside of or beyond the tidy linearities that reason insists upon.

Alexander, a generation older than these enthusiasts, tries to be a moderating influence, but he too will be swept off his feet by events that he and his younger fellow-Russians encourage, witness, and experience. He reasonably insists: "Philosophy consists in moderating each life so that many lives will fit together with as much liberty and justice as will keep them together – and not so much as will make them fly apart" (23). His point is a good one, but it is one that presumes an ability to control the uncontrollable. The trilogy is an extended lesson demonstrating Alexander's tragic misunderstanding of the uncontrollable forces of human nature and unpredictable nature of human history.

Into this dreamy mix of philosophy students, literary critics, and struggling journalists steps Herzen, revolutionary, a man who decries the various moony concepts of revolution, including the point that literature is revolutionary. For him, "We're not the plaything of an imaginative cosmic force, but of a Romanov [the Tsar] with no imagination whatsoever, a mediocrity" (105). We need to remember that even as the serfs are oppressed by Russia's feudal system, so is everyone else oppressed by the monarchic police state that is nineteenth-century Russia. Herzen calls for action by insisting that "to rail against the march of history was pointless and self-important, to deplore the unfortunate details was pedantic, and for art to concern itself was ridiculous" (104). He argues that

"Hegel's Dialectical Spirit of History" got it all wrong, just as these lounge-chair radicals have gotten it all wrong: "People don't storm the Bastille because history proceeds by zigzags. History zigzags because when people have had enough, they storm the Bastille" (104). He adds that this whole Hegelian philosophical insistence that history is inevitable is "an extravagant redundancy even if one could imagine what sort of animal it was supposed to be … a gigantic ginger cat, for example" (104).

Are the forces of history pushing humanity to inevitable outcomes? That is the question Stoppard leaves us with at the end of *Part One*.

Part two: *Shipwreck*

> The mistake is to put our ideas before action. Act first.
> The ideas will follow, and if not – well, it's progress.   *The Coast of*
> *Utopia*, Part Two: *Shipwreck* (36)

All the talk, theorizing, and idle romancing – and most of the enthusiasm – dissipate in *Shipwreck*, where ideas take the form of action with cataclysmic results. Alexander Herzen, "would-be revolutionary," now takes centerstage, along with his wife, Natalie. They become the epicenter that the Bakunin family was in *Part One*, and it is clearly a different, far more activist world.

Once again, Stoppard combines world events with domestic affairs. In *Part Two*, we have revolution, cataclysm, and loss unraveling around Herzen both in world affairs and personally, including the anxieties that attend having a deaf son and numerous sickly, forlorn friends. Included as one of his burdens is Ivan Turgenev, whose desperate love for an opera singer who treats him with utter contempt embroils everyone to a certain degree. Romantic strains – emotional and philosophical – flower the play, offering a mix of bright-eyed optimism and "Byronic" self-pity.

The main problem is that these high-minded Russian thinkers, artists, revolutionaries have lost touch with the world about them as they pursue intellectual abstractions. We actually hear that they have entered into the European lexicon as "intelligentsia," defined as "A uniquely Russian phenomenon, the intellectual opposition considered as a social force" (15).[7] They are all currently infatuated with Paris and all things French, much as they were infatuated with German philosophy in *Part One*. A self-described "slavophile," Aksakov, attacks his fellows for falling for the Western model, which he calls little more than a "bourgeois monarchy for philistines and profiteers" (12). He calls his circle of revolutionary wannabes "Jacobins and German sentimentalists. Destroyers and dreamers," adding, "You've turned your back

12 *The Coast of Utopia: Shipwreck.* Directed by Jack O'Brien.
Standing: Ethan Hawke (Michael Bakunin); Jason Butler Harner (Ivan
Turgenev), Bianca Amato (Emma Herwegh). Vivian Beaumont Theater
at Lincoln Center, 2006

on your own people, the real Russians abandoned a hundred and fifty years ago
by Peter the Great Westerniser!" (12). He argues that intellectuals need to
"reunite . . . with the masses from whom we became separated when we put on
silk breeches and powdered wigs" (13). Aksakov goes too far, however, in that
he has simply become another type of romantic, seeing "the Russian way" as
the "true path" to a glorious future. His point about getting back to the ground
floor and connecting with the material world – the masses certainly included –
is something everyone seems to agree with but also something no one knows
how to do.

Prolonged debate and indecision call into question exactly how history
unfolds. After every revolution in *Part Two* ends in "shipwreck," Herzen won-
ders: "We note the haphazard chaos of history by the day, by the hour, but there
is something wrong with the picture. Where is the unity, the meaning, of nature's
highest creation?" (101). The problem of meaning and unity and sense is the
problem that pervades the entire trilogy. Herzen summarizes it aptly:

> Where are we off to? Who's got the map? We study the ideal societies . . .
> power to the experts, to the workers, to the philosophers . . . property
> rights, property sanctions, the evil of competition, the evil of monopoly,

central planning, free housing, free love … limited to eight hundred families or unconstrained by national frontiers … and all of them uniquely harmonious, just and efficient.   (16)

Herzen does have his preferences, of course: "I'm not saying socialism is history's secret plan, it just looks like the rational step" (17). But even though it appears that "the future is being scrawled on the factory walls of Paris" (17), history does not progress rationally, and if Herzen's dream of a socialist utopia is ever to be achieved, it will not arrive in any rational, logical, or sensible way.

One might expect the re-entrance of an enthusiastic Michael Bakunin to signal the arrival of unexpected changes. But he is a case of dreaming gone completely off the deep end, romantically captivating and almost childishly alluring in his naivete, believing as he does that "the Tsar and all his works will be gone within a year, or two at the most," and insisting, "forget about the French. Polish independence is the only revolutionary spark in Europe" (31). To be fair, his revolutionary spirit holds true even under torture and threat of execution, a giant of a man in a world too small for his dreams.

Michael Bakunin stands in contrast to the more reasonable Herzen, whose fondness for Bakunin is nonetheless unqualified. But when Bakunin says things like "Freedom is a state of mind," Herzen responds with, "No, it's a state of not being locked up" (35). Curiously, though, when Bakunin is locked up and interrogated in Dresden, he does behave as if freedom were a state of mind, verifying the dreamer's right to exist because of the inspiration he generates for the rest of us. But one at least senses that in the end pragmatists like Herzen are the ones who quietly improve the world. Herzen's sensibility and confidence draw us into his way of thinking, but he soon discovers that his control is illusory. He is unable to spare his family death and suffering, and he is unable to do anything to prevent the cataclysm of failed revolutions that will sweep across Europe.

The play moves to March 1848, a month after the fall of the French king Louis Philippe, with Bakunin declaring he had finally met someone "from the working class" (39) and Karl Marx declaring after-the-fact that the revolution "was bound to happen" (38). One enthusiast, the radical poet George Herwegh, buys six hundred train tickets and leads "a brigade of German Democratic Exiles" (40) to the German frontier to spark his own revolution. Bakunin is in his element, shouting out, "This is what it was all for, from the beginning … studying Kant, Schelling, Fichte" (42), and Turgenev is likewise swept away, helping Marx find the right word for his manifesto: "A *spirit* … a spirit is haunting Europe" (42).

And then the shock: "The Provisional Government promised elections. Elections took place. Nine million Frenchmen voted for the first time. Well, they voted royalists, rentiers, lawyers … and a rump of socialists for the rest to

13 *The Coast of Utopia: Shipwreck*. Directed by Jack O'Brien. Left to right: Ethan Hawke (Michael Bakunin), Adam Dannheisser (Karl Marx). Vivian Beaumont Theater at Lincoln Center, 2006

kick" (46). The masses, the workers, it appears, were not ready for revolution and basically voted for a return to the status quo. Doomed efforts to build barricades against counterrevolution lead to bloodshed and a return to monarchy. And neither were the Germans ready for change: Herwegh returns in disgrace. The hope that Tsarist Russia would fall is hardly imaginable at this point. Herzen observes, "Well, now we know what the reactionaries have always known: liberty, equality, and fraternity are like three rotten apples in their barrel of privilege, even a pip could prove fatal" (54). In other words, the power elite know that even small advances would lead to their personal ruin and cannot be tolerated. So Herzen concludes, "From now on it's all or nothing, no quarter, no mercy" (54). The problem is that through all of this, Herzen and others discover that the leaders of the various revolutionary governments-in-exile are small-minded, uninspiring, and underqualified. Hope dims measurably as the play progresses.

Herzen idolized Rousseau's rights-of-man philosophy, as did many in his circle. But the revolution of the people is undermined by the very people such a change was meant to benefit. Belinsky speaks for many when he says, "I'm sick of utopias," adding, "I'd trade the whole lot for one practical difference that owes nothing to anybody's ideal society, one commonsensical action that puts right an injury to one person" (55). Dreaming has turned to more pragmatic things, including, as Belinsky does, celebrating the completion of "the railway station in St. Petersburg" (56). He calls it "the poetry of practical gesture" (56).

George Herwegh's hard-earned lessons lead to a similar point, aptly summarizing this intelligentsia's experience with the real world:

> We discovered that history has no respect for intellectuals. History is more like the weather. You never know what it's going to do. God, we were busy! – bustling about under the sky, shouting directions to the winds, remonstrating with the clouds in German, Russian, French … and hailing every sunbeam as proof of the power of words.   (63)

The Coast of Utopia in general is Stoppard's demonstration that humanity is not the power it thinks itself to be. Putting Karl Marx and his *Communist Manifesto* into the picture is a mere hint – but an important one – that future shipwrecks are in the offing.

Two old friends, Maria and Natalie, move the big ideas into another sphere as they discuss love. Natalie continues to believe that "our sex is ennobled by idealizing love" (68), which Maria rejects, observing that following the break-up of her "ideal" first marriage, she fell in love with an artist, and "it stank of turpentine, tobacco smoke, laundry baskets." Her conclusion: "To arouse and satisfy desire is nature making its point about the sexes, everything else is convention" (69). Natalie attacks Maria's descent into mere carnality and criticizes the talents of Maria's lover as "neither art nor love" (70) by pointing out what many of Stoppard's other characters have said for years: "Imitation isn't art … Technique by itself can't create" (70). What Stoppard offers at this point is an earthy and vulgar nude portrait of Maria. Realism untouched by idealism is vulgar at best, a good definition for pornography. Shortly thereafter Stoppard includes another nude portrait, this one of Natalie (arranged in the manner of Manet's "Luncheon on the Grass"). But neither disputant fully realizes the point that this latter painting makes, namely that art is where reality and idealism creatively interact. It is a painting that implicitly asks whether the combination can exist anywhere other than in art.

In fact, when Natalie tries to move her idealist theories about art into the real world, husband Herzen refuses to accept that her affair with George Herwegh (for whom the painting is destined) is noble and honorable, miserably ending her attempt to bring the ideal into the real world. And her world in general is further shattered when news arrives of a literal shipwreck: their young deaf son drowns at sea. Natalie, we hear, dies of grief three months later. Reality crushes idealism at virtually every turn.

In the next-to-last scene Herzen is on a ship headed for England, and Bakunin's spirit meets him at a deck rail. Bakunin remains undaunted, determined that revolution will prevail. Thinking of the short, simple life of his drowned son, Herzen observes: "Nature doesn't disdain what lives for a *day*. It pours the whole of itself into each moment ... Life's bounty is in its flow, later is too late. Where is the song when it's been sung? The dance when it's been danced?" (101). Waxing poetic, but hitting a key point in this play, Herzen observes:

> Surely those millions of little streams of accident and willfulness have their correction in the vast underground river which, without a doubt, is carrying us to the place where we're expected! But there is no such place, that's why it's called utopia. The death of a child has no more meaning than the death of armies, of nations. Was a child happy while he lived? That is a proper question, the only question. If we can't arrange our own happiness, it's a conceit beyond vulgarity to arrange the happiness of those who come after us.   (101)

Theories and ideals mean nothing if they do not improve the moment. Life is to be lived, and the order that nature creates will be an order that will occur regardless of our interventions. Herzen moves up to the grand scheme of things when he announces: "In the west, socialism may win next time, but it is not history's destination. Socialism, too, will reach its own extremes and absurdities, and once more Europe will burst at the seams" (104). So claims Herzen.

Herzen's points actually ironically identify Bakunin as the one man who has lived an authentic, full life, savoring each moment as he slugs forward with dreams and hopes. His vitality, not his vision (or anyone else's), is the most impressive thing in this play.

The final scene returns us to the play's opening scene, offering an invitation for us to reflect back and measure the successes of the various dreamers and their results thus far.

Part Three: Salvage

> A distant end is not an end but a trap.   *The Coast of Utopia, Part Three:*
> *Salvage* (119)

Opening with a scene of domestic quiet, *Salvage* plays with the idea of repetition, since it nearly duplicates the scene of domestic order that opens *Part One*. Instead of Alexander Bakunin as patriarch, however, Alexander Herzen is patriarch, though he is only forty years old. It is 1853, and the revolutionary fire exists almost exclusively in theory at this point. We hear that "Marx is always getting thrown out of pubs by the English workingman" (5), and we are introduced to a band of exiles from numerous countries on the continent. Herzen's home is a comfortable refuge in London for all sorts of dreamers and parasites.

All the exiles seem a bit mystified by British life, with socialist-in-exile Blanc observing (in a manner reminiscent of Mr. Moon in Stoppard's novel):

> They have the ridiculous idea they're the most advanced nation
> on earth, but they haven't discovered the principle of organization.
> Everything here is connected in some incomprehensible sideways
> manner, instead of top to bottom like in a sensible country. There's no
> system to anything – society, the law, literary life – everything's just
> left to grow tangled together.   (12)

But then Blanc goes on to talk about the British love of "shrooberies" and gardening in general, harkening back to *Arcadia* and the idea that the free-flowing irregular style of landscaping aptly reflects the nineteenth-century British sensibility. Somehow, inexplicably, things work out in Britain, presumably thanks to that thing called "liberty." As Herzen points out about the British, "They invented personal liberty, and they know it, and they did it without having any theories about it" (12). Later, an old revolutionary asks, "Do poverty and liberty go together, or is it the English sense of humour?" (78), the implicit answer to both questions being "Yes."

14 *The Coast of Utopia: Salvage.* Directed by Jack O'Brien.
Brian F. O'Byrne (Alexander Herzen) and cast. Vivian Beaumont
Theater at Lincoln Center, 2006

Herzen is a crushed man, though he still rather romantically embraces his disillusion:

> I came to Paris as people used to come to Jerusalem or Rome, and found the city of the plain. It made one half-hearted effort to be worthy of itself and then collapsed satisfied under six feet of dung, not even brimstone. I have lost every illusion dear to me. I'm forty. I will dwell in the land of Nod, to the east of Eden, and the world will hear no more of me.   (16)

Almost instantly, however, he comes alive at the suggestion that he organize a free Russian and Polish press in London, trusting once again to the power of language and ideas to enact change.

His is an optimism that at long last almost seems justified when news arrives that the tyrant Tsar Nicholas has died and has been replaced by his more tolerant son. Herzen's literary enterprises may ultimately have had some effect because we hear of Russia's emancipation of the serfs. But the emancipation becomes little more than a title change because the freed serfs are still bound to the land for subsistence and the land still belongs to the old landowners. It is a victory with limited consequences, as Natalie points out: "nothing belongs to them and they have to pay rent for their plots ... obviously freedom bears an uncanny resemblance to serfdom" (90). Freedom without literally real grounding is an empty idealism.

Then, amid celebration muted by suspicion of ultimate failure, in rushes Bakunin, "*a huge and hirsute force, an emperor of tramp*" just arrived from a bold and adventurous circumnavigational escape from political prison. Hearing that all fronts have gone quiet throughout Europe, Bakunin bellows, "Good Christ, it's lucky I'm back" (92). The catapulting energy of boundless idealism seems to have its place in the world after all.

As noted earlier, Karl Marx exists in the play as a persistent bit of background noise. We know, of course, that this man will rise in fame beyond any of the central characters in the trilogy, spouting such pronouncements as, "Every stage leads to a higher stage in the permanent conflict which is the march of history" (118), adding that once "Capital and Labour stand revealed in fatal contradiction":

> Then will come the final titanic struggle, the last turn of the great wheel of progress beneath which generations of toiling masses perished for the ultimate victory. Now at last the unity and rationality of history's purpose will be clear to everyone ... Everything that seemed vicious, mean, and ugly, the broken lives and ignoble deaths of millions, will be understood as part of a higher reality, a superior morality, against which resistance is irrational – a cosmos where every

atom has been striving for the goal of human self-realisation and the culmination of history.　(118–19)

But Alexander Herzen, having fully experienced a life of love, sacrifice, and death, contradicts Marx's fully mechanistic, utterly non-human vision:

> But history has no culmination … History knocks at a thousand gates at every moment, and the gatekeeper is chance. We shout into the mist for this one or that one to be opened for us, but through every gate there are a thousand more. We need wit and courage to make our way while our way is making us. But that is our dignity as human beings, and we rob ourselves if we pardon us by the absolution of historical necessity.　(119)

Humanity is faced with an almost infinite number of choices as it confronts an unpredictability that looms before us all. For Herzen this is sobering but by no means tragic news.

Then there is Michael Bakunin's anarchist response. He utterly indulges his urges with a lust that stands out as unadulterated *joie de vivre*, even (or especially) as he suffers incarceration and exile. Through all of his misadventures, Bakunin offers a boisterous summation of existence: "Seven degrees of human happiness! First, to die fighting for liberty; second, love and friendship; third, art and science; fourth a cigarette; fifth, drinking; sixth, eating; and seventh, sleeping" (117). Bakunin reveals that living is the attraction that Marx has left out of his formula.

In *Salvage*, Stoppard has his anarchist wild man Bakunin rewrite the story of the Garden of Eden as follows:

> Once – long ago, at the beginning of history – we were all free. Man was at one with his nature, and so he was good. He was in harmony with the world. Conflict was unknown. Then the serpent entered the garden, and the name of the serpent was – Order. Social organisation! The world was no longer at one with itself. Matter and spirit divided. Man was no longer whole. He was driven by ambition, acquisitiveness, jealousy, fear … Conflict became the condition of his life, the individual against his neighbour, against society, against himself. The Golden Age was ended.　(35)

Bakunin then asks and answers: "How can we make a new Golden Age and set men free again? By destroying everything that destroyed their freedom" (35). Stoppard puts this speech in the mouth of the most irresponsibly seductive character he has yet created. He uses Bakunin as a sophisticated court jester who refuses to worry about reprisal or consequence for his thoughts and actions. His bold, heroic, and even romantic lack of fear makes even his craziest thoughts worth paying attention to.

If Bakunin is one extreme and Marx another, Herzen arrives at a point somewhere in between though much closer to Bakunin than to Marx. Quietly, nearing exhaustion but not resignation, Bakunin observes, "We have to open men's eyes and not tear them out ... and if we see differently, it's all right, we don't have to kill the myopic in our myopia ... We have to bring what's good along with us" (119–20). And he speaks for immediate results: "A distant end is not an end but a trap. The end we work for must be closer, the labourer's wage, the pleasure in the work done, the summer lightning of personal happiness" (119).

Even though the events in *The Coast of Utopia* document historical but obscure Russian and European intellectuals from the nineteenth century, their obscurity does not hide the fact that – historically speaking – their lives will end in disappointment. They are, after all, the well-intended precursors to the great twentieth-century cataclysm known as Soviet Communism. But watching the trilogy goes beyond this intellectual fact. Watching the train wreck unfold before our eyes does far more than simply tell us what happened. Stoppard fast-forwards and reverses action throughout the trilogy in a manner reminiscent of many of his other plays' structures, and as we move back and forth, we carry with us an awareness of what is around the corner. As the fragments all come together, we grow increasingly aware of a pattern unfolding before us, in a fractal manner first introduced in *Arcadia*. It begs us to consider that in the unraveling sequences that are our lives, perhaps there is a rhythm and pattern as well, not reductively linear as we might like, but rich and complexly varied. Forcing existence into predetermined channels destroys the potential that stands before us and before humanity in general.

Rock'n'Roll: the real revolution of the spirit

> We have to rediscover our human mystery in the age of technology.   *Rock'n'Roll* (47)

Cambridge and Prague, 1968 to 1990, tutorials on Sappho, translations of ancient Greek and Latin texts, Pan, political debates, Pink Floyd, breast cancer, the Rolling Stones, family life, police-state brutality, Plastic People of the Universe, Syd Barrett. Michael Billington sums up the overall effect of *Rock'n'Roll* when he calls it "above all a celebration of the pagan spirit embodied by rock'n'roll."[8] And Clive Barnes reports: "Just as 'The Coast of Utopia' took as its canvas a portrait of the nineteenth century seen through the camera lens of a group of Russian intellectuals, Stoppard has now focused the same lens, the same dramatic process, on his own time. And it's now even more sharply focused."[9] If *Rock'n'Roll* is a streamlined version of *The Coast of Utopia*, it is also a work that connects equally substantively with many of Stoppard's earlier works.

Again alternating between two worlds – Cambridge and Prague – and two time periods – pre- and post-Velvet Revolution – *Rock'n'Roll* mainly follows Czech underground resistance to Communist oppression beginning in 1968, leading to a new Eastern European democracy initiated by the 1989 "velvet" collapse of Czech Communism. In this regard, the work taps into Stoppard's earlier Eastern European works, like *Neutral Ground, Professional Foul*, and *Squaring the Circle*, though *Rock'n'Roll* has the benefit of time to reflect in ways its predecessors could not.

Beneath the central political struggle for freedom, Stoppard inserts two unlikely creative forces. One is the mysterious character The Piper – also called Pan – who later turns out to be Syd Barrett, the once irrepressible heart of the band Pink Floyd. The other is the Czech band Plastic People of the Universe, bent on playing rock'n'roll without any regard to political pressure or personal fame. As the play unfolds, what becomes evident is that Barrett and the Plastic People are manifestations of the spirit of anarchic emancipation, utterly disregarding social forces surrounding them and asking simply to be permitted to live. The irony is that they turn out to be politically far more dangerous than actual activists because they have no interest in politics and therefore are unaffected by the oppressively conformist machinations of prevailing social forces. As one character, Jan, notes, "Policemen *love* dissidents like the Inquisition loved heretics. Heretics give meaning to the defenders of the faith" (37), adding that when dissidents confront the state, the state has already won because at that point everyone is playing the game by the "house rules" that the state has created. The only way to beat the house is to not play its game.

Non-players for the most part, Barrett and The Plastic People remain an undercurrent throughout the play. The suggestion is that politics at its heart is an incomplete exercise striving for something that can only be achieved by other more fundamental means. Ferdinand, a dissident turned tune-out convert, summarizes why bands like The Plastic People, and their supporters, are actually such dangerous forces. First the censors suggest, "'Cut your hair just a little, and we'll let you play.' Then the tempter says, 'Just change the name of the band and you can play.' And after that, 'Just leave out this one song.'" To avoid entrapment of any sort, he says, "It is better not to start by cutting your hair" because "Then nothing you do can possibly give support to the idea that everything is in order in this country" (39). The point is eerily reminiscent of America's own 1960s when the status quo was undermined by a youth movement that tuned out and embraced an extended, rock-inspired summer of love. On the surface, political activism gets the credit for whatever changes eventuated (such as the end of the Vietnam war). But a closer look may reveal that change might never have happened had it not been for the freewheeling British and American rock'n'roll energy behind the political movement.

Then, too, the play also reminds us of the painful shortcomings and incompleteness that attend the pursuit of utopian dreams. Much like the French Revolution of 1848 in *The Coast of Utopia*, the Velvet Revolution that is so central to *Rock'n'Roll* falls short of its utopian potential and instead paves the way for Western individualist self-centeredness to colonize newly liberated Eastern Europe. For the Czech Republic in 1990, the character Jan is right to say, "These are new times. Who will be rich? Who will be famous?" (107), accurately seeing the dream for a more perfect union replaced by capitalist and individualist self-indulgence.

But there is more to this play than a history lesson on Eastern Bloc politics and debates about political activism and its discontents. Max is an unrepentant Communist Party member, a Czech expatriate teaching at Cambridge University and serving initially as that institution's cultural curiosity: the last committed Communist in the Western world. He has witnessed all his

15 *Rock'n'Roll*. Directed by Trevor Nunn. Left to right: Brian Cox (Max), Rufus Sewell (Jan). Jerwood Theatre Downstairs/Royal Court Theatre, London, 2006

Communist/Marxist ideals compromised or simply abandoned by war, invasion, oligarchic greed, and downright acts of evil. Yet he still believes the Marxist dictum, "from each according to ability, to each according to need," asking, "What could be more simple, more rational, more beautiful?" (25). Max's beleaguered protégé, Jan, offers an answer:

> Perhaps we aren't good enough for this beautiful idea. This is the best we can do with it. Marx knew we couldn't be trusted. First the dictatorship, till we learned to be good, then the utopia where a man can be a baker in the morning, a lawmaker in the afternoon and a poet in the evening. But we never learned to be good, so look at us. (25)

Jan's description is a fair description of Athenian life during the famous Periclean Age of Athens (450–430 BC), when the ideals of democracy, the community, and "the whole man" flourished, as described, for a sadly brief period.

It is entirely possible that Jan is self-consciously alluding to the Greeks in this passage, given that Greek literature directly finds its way into the play through Eleanor, Max's wife. She is a classical Greek scholar whose tutorials with her students include the erotic love poetry of Sappho. Controlling the means of production is a popular Marxist demand, which for Max is more important to the idea of freedom than anything else. But it seems, too, that Eleanor's love-centered Greek ideals must have some bearing on the nature of freedom, clashing with Max's Marxist materialism.

This conflict is translated into the couple's married life. It is exacerbated by two personal issues: Max is an amoral philanderer and Eleanor is physically wasting away as a result of breast cancer. Both matters trigger questions about the physical versus spiritual nature of life. For example, given that their seemingly incompatible relationship survives against all reason, there must be some "spark" between the two that transcends material explanation, but Max for all the world will not buy into this non-rational foolishness. As a proper Marxist materialist and atheist, he cannot accept anything that is not materially certifiable. Eleanor, on the other hand, begins with a belief that life and love are transcendent realities, though her struggle with her dying body leads her to suspect that love, passion, eros might actually be bodily responses after all: "My body is telling me I'm nothing without it, and you're telling me the same" (50). If body is everything, then Eleanor is slowly but surely disappearing, a point she can't accept, screaming out, "*I am not my body*. My body is nothing without *me*" (51).

Max works to comfort her by saying he loves her mind, but Eleanor will not have it since she knows that Max's vision of mind is that it is just some biological machine: "I want your grieving soul or nothing. I do not want your amazing biological machine – I want what you love me with" (51).

Max's reply is tender, but he sticks to his guns: "But that's what I love you with. That's it. There's nothing else" (51). For Max everything is physically rooted. Eleanor longs for something more transcendent.

Eleanor dies, and her daughter Esme grows up, remembering her ill-spent youth while she raises her own daughter under the watchful eye of grandfather Max. Esme seems to be a failure in all things except raising her daughter. She had the qualifications to enter Cambridge University but chose to join a commune instead. She fell in love and had a child but her husband left her. She is currently helping her aging father recover from a broken leg, and her daughter is about to enter Cambridge in her own right.

Much to Max's despair – much as with the revolutionaries in *The Coast of Utopia* – there is the lingering frustration that the masses are not the "noble" class of humans he would like them to be. About Britain, for example, Max observes that "the working-class vote could make this a socialist country *permanently*, and they voted in the millions for the most reactionary Tory government of modern times" (81). What is it the masses want? "They eat crap, they read crap, they watch crap, they have two weeks in the sun, and they're content" (81). Stephen offers the history lesson Max will not accept: "Marx read his Darwin but he missed it. Capitalism doesn't self-destruct, it adapts" (81), giving the people basically what they want. The adaptation generates less than they could demand but is suitable for contentment. Stephen insists that it is the way of the world, and it will undermine even the great "populist" reversals in Soviet-controlled Eastern Europe. Marxism ultimately crumbles under its own materialist/economic inefficiencies, replaced by another system of materialism that indulges the selfish human urge for individual gain.

Max the wizened patriarch at the end of the play offers his view of the world in its recent pursuit of liberty: "The fifties was the last time liberty opened up as you left your youth behind you. After that, young people started off with more liberty than they knew what to do with ... but – regrettably – confused it with sexual liberation and the freedom to get high ... so it all went to waste" (95). Genuine liberty has a limited life span, it appears. It quickly degenerates into individualized indulgence. What Stoppard reminds us is that with the triumph of capitalist good over totalitarian evil, we are left with the banality of asking, "Who will be rich? Who will be famous?" (107). Real matters of justice and equity have been abandoned. Even a charismatic hero like President Václav Havel cannot keep his nation focused on such high ideals. For better or worse, freedom boils down to something far less than humanity dreams of achieving.

What the play gives us toward its end are several uncomfortable resolutions. Max's family seems more or less settled into modest comfort. Max and his protégé, Jan, reconcile. Esme accepts Jan's offer to go away with him to Prague, confirming they have been in love for many years. Esme's daughter Alice will go to Cambridge University, and her father will marry fellow "journalist" Candida. No fan of Candida's career, Max notes that current journalism should be embarrassed to do what it does after the legacy of real journalism. But that is only a minor point among a laundry list of things that have not gone quite right but are a long way from being as bad as they used to be.

The last scene combines Cambridge and Prague in a mix reminiscent of *Arcadia*'s conclusion. Lenka, the student of many years ago, is now at Cambridge teaching what Max's wife Eleanor once taught. Eleanor's grand-daughter Alice is learning Greek and Latin, reading the tragic text that announces the death of Pan: "and there was a great cry of lamentation, not one voice but many" (107). Lenka holds to her liberal ideals even to the end, arguing with Max that "you think human nature is a beast which must be put in a cage. But it is the cage that makes the animal bad" (100). Max counters, more philosophically: "The cage is reason" (101), insisting that it is a necessary instrument to prevent humanity from losing self-control. Lenka says that reason is Max's "superstition." She does not accept Max's position.

And neither does Stoppard, finally, accept Max's position, but it is not because of Max's Marxism. It is because of Max's uncompromising materialist rationalism. For Stoppard, the cluttered, complex, but genuine family that he puts onstage works not because of rationalism but actually against all reason. There is something more to existence than the material here-and-now, which in its way is paradoxically among the worst kinds of idealism. In the case of *Rock'n'Roll* there is a *spirit* that binds a family together. We clearly sense its existence even in the face of rationalist and materialist denials. This seems to be Stoppard's lament. Pan is dead, or nearly so, in the play, replaced by a materialist worship of personal gain. Syd Barrett still ambles through the back alleys of Cambridge, a curiosity that is more like an endangered species. Lust for living free of monetary, political, or ideological obsession is something that shot momentary beams into our consciousnesses but faded the moment the possibility could have become manifest.

Conclusion: The play's the thing

The notes, the notes! The notes is where the fun is!   *Indian Ink* (4)

In a 2001 assessment, Enoch Brater observes that Stoppard's "best stage effects depend on an audience 'there' to meet him (at least) half way."[1] Brater then asks the question that likely haunts many theatregoers as they enter Stoppard's theatre and cast glances at fellow patrons taking seats around them: "Just how specialized ... is Stoppard's audience?" (212).

Going to a Stoppard play, I suggest, does become a richer experience if we bring some degree of expertise with us to the theatre. But it is not the case that we need to be university dons in order to enjoy the plays that Stoppard spices with such intellectual esoterica as quantum physics, nineteenth-century European history, chaotics, catastrophe theory, literary theory, logical positivism, life at Elsinore Castle. Stoppard himself goes so far as to declare that his plays are stand-alone experiences. When asked if he had any advice to give on approaching his plays, he responded: "the plays declare themselves and there is nothing I want to add to the experience. I am not claiming any mystique for understanding the plays, so I can't demystify them. They're supposed to work just by being what they are, and I don't think of them as being 'difficult.'"[2] Not everyone would entirely agree with his assessment, though it may in fact be true that we would enjoy Stoppard's work more fully if we stopped worrying about the many peripheral factual details that occupy so much space in his theatre.

But for many of us, there still remains the curious desire to move into the footnote world of his plays, perhaps because factuality gives us something to grasp as we move through Stoppard's fascinating sea of uncertainties. There are numerous examples of unasked-for editorial assistance from among Stoppard's audiences. For example, one scholar wrote to Stoppard to let him know that Fourier's prize 1811 essay could not possibly have reached England by 1812 (consider the obstacle of the Napoleonic Wars), contrary to events in *Arcadia*. Another pointed out that Sadi Carnot (of entropy fame) was only 16 in 1812, and his famous essay "Réflexions sur la puissance motrice du feu"

("Reflections on the Motive Power of Fire") was not published until 1824. Others have noted that including a waltz in *Arcadia* is toying with chronology as well. True or not, is any of this relevant to the pleasure of *Arcadia* proper? And what about *Shakespeare in Love*? One historian pointed out that the colony of Virginia was not settled until after Elizabeth's reign. Similar conflicts with factuality surface in numerous works throughout Stoppard's canon. Some are by design, others are perhaps genuine mistakes.

But this sort of "meeting Stoppard half way" is not Brater's point. Rather, perhaps more in line with Brater's intended meaning, there are the cases of specialists who appreciate Stoppard's theatre precisely because they understand what he is doing with the specialized material at hand. It's not the factuality so much as what Stoppard does with the factuality. Cambridge don, particle physicist, and Anglican priest J. C. Polkinghorne – a specialist if ever there was one – corresponded with Stoppard and expressed how much he enjoyed the wild connections presented in the physics-laden *Hapgood*. Noted philosopher A. J. Ayer responded likewise about *Jumpers*, and so did chaotician Robert M. May about *Arcadia*. What these men see is Stoppard leaping and bounding from one discipline to another, and the results are new levels of understanding manufactured by endless combinations and recombinations. The genius lies in the interconnectivity.

So what is it we should bring to a Stoppard play? In the final analysis, Stoppard's plays are enterprises that encourage us to experience multiple perspectives, points of view, and levels of satisfaction. And though they can be appreciated as stand-alone products, the Stoppard experience can be enhanced by a certain degree of preparation – as this book has endeavored to demonstrate. So, when next anticipating a Stoppard play, before the lights go down, recall a thing or two about Stoppard that you read prior to the play. Then look over the program notes. But above all, turn to the play proper, open your eyes and mind, and enjoy.

Appendix: Stoppard's theatre: a summary

> But these are merely the facts.   *The Invention of Love* (95)

The Gamblers was written in 1960 and given a single production at the Bristol Old Vic Theatre School by a Bristol University student group in 1965.

It is a play involving a condemned political prisoner and his jailer. By the end of their extended conversation the two men change roles, and the jailer goes to his death.

A Walk on the Water was written in 1960 and rewritten as a 90-minute television play (broadcast by Rediffusion, November 1963). As a translated work entitled *Der Spleen des George Riley*, it became Stoppard's first fully staged play on June 30, 1964, in Hamburg, Germany. This work eventually became *Enter a Free Man*. See below.

The Dissolution of Dominic Boot. This 15-minute radio play was broadcast in a BBC series called *Just Before Midnight*, February 1964. Converted to a mini-film in 1969 called *The Engagement*, it aired on American television and in British cinemas in 1970.

A young man in a hired cab is forced to drive through the city to find enough money from friends and other sources to pay his cab fare. The more he looks the deeper in debt he becomes, until he is utterly destitute.

"M" is for Moon among Other Things. Originally a short story published in *Introduction II: Stories by New Writers* (London: Faber & Faber, 1962), this 15-minute radio play was broadcast in early 1964 in the BBC series *Just Before Midnight*.

A loveless middle-aged couple finds meaning in various ways: Alfred looks for sensational stories in the newspaper, musing about how he might have been able to save Marilyn Monroe (who died in 1962); Constance, obsessed with order and possessed of a good memory, is reading an encyclopedia purchased volume-to-volume on installment. She is currently reading volume M–N.

If You're Glad I'll be Frank, a radio play, was broadcast by BBC's Third Programme on February 8, 1966, commissioned for a program on non-existent jobs called *Strange Occupations*. It was converted for the stage in 1969.

Gladys is the "speaking clock," the phone voice for the correct-time dial-up. She is obsessed with how time regiments modern life. Tom, her husband, is a bus driver. He tries to get Gladys to break her obsession. Caught up with his own time-schedule (and his bus conductress's insistence), he fails to save Gladys (or himself), and Gladys continues on as the speaking clock.

A Separate Peace. This 30-minute television play aired on BBC 2, August 1966, paired with a documentary by Stoppard and Christopher Brown on chess players. Directed by Alan Gibson.

A perfectly healthy John Brown checks himself into a nursing home in order to escape the chaos of the world. The employees try everything to remove him, but he charmingly persists, painting murals on the hospital ward halls, until the staff locates his family. On the eve of the family coming for him, he quietly leaves the hospital.

Teeth. This 30-minute television play aired February 7, 1967 on the BBC, starring John Stride and John Wood, directed by Alan Gibson.

A dentist gets to exact revenge against a patient who has had an affair with his wife, ruining his teeth and cuckolding the cuckolder in the process.

Another Moon Called Earth. This 30-minute television play aired in June 1967, starring John Wood and Alan Bennett, directed by Alan Gibson.

Bone, a historian, seeks patterns in human existence. The project has progressed only up to the Greeks of the third century BC. His flirtatious wife Penelope has lost her moral center as she witnesses the first lunar landing on television. Her doctor, Albert, seems to have been taking advantage of his patient, though upon reflection everything appears to be in proper order. Inspector Crouch enters, announcing the death – or suicide – of a woman, fallen from the apartment building's heights. Nothing is resolved; everything is suggested.

Albert's Bridge. Part of BBC's Third Programme, this radio play aired July 13, 1967, winning the Prix Italia Award. John Hurt played Albert. The play was later converted for the stage and performed by the Oxford Theatre Group at Edinburgh, 1969, and at the King's Head, London in 1976.

Albert is a quiet, reserved former college philosophy student who takes a job on a work crew painting the Clufton Bay Bridge rather than joining his father in the family firm of Metal Alloys and Allied Metals. When the city decides to economize, Albert becomes sole bridge painter, beginning again as soon as the task is completed. Albert loves the rhythm and life cycle of his job, and he loves the peaceful, patterned perspective on the world that he gets from the bridge's heights. But this obsession destroys his life on the ground with his wife, family, and everyone else. When it is revealed that the city planners have miscalculated, leaving the bridge exposed and rusting at one end while Albert does his job at the other end, the city hires 1,799 workers to paint the bridge in a day, destroying Albert's rhythm, happiness, and – because of the miscalculated weight of the workers – the bridge itself.

Rosencrantz and Guildenstern Are Dead derives from the earlier one-act verse comedy *Rosencrantz and Guildenstern Meet King Lear*. It premiered in Cranston Street Hall in Edinburgh at the Fringe of Edinburgh Festival, August 24, 1966, by the Oxford Theatre Group. The professional premiere was at the Old Vic Theatre, London, April 11, 1967, by the National Theatre, starring John Stride and Edward Petherbridge, directed by Derek Goldby. Stoppard won the John Whiting Award (with Wole Soyinka), *Plays and Players* Best Play Award, and *Evening Standard* Award for Most Promising Playwright (with David Storey). Its New York premiere was at the Alvin Theatre, October 16, 1967, starring Brian Murray and John Wood, directed by Derek Goldby. It won the Tony Award and Drama Critics' Circle Award for Best Play.

Two minor characters from Shakespeare's *Hamlet* are thrust into a world of uncertainty. Matters of probability, certainty, and the way the world operates become the things that obsess these two characters as they also try to figure out what their purpose is in the world and in Hamlet's Elsinore castle. They go to their deaths as the script of *Hamlet* ordains.

Lord Malquist and Mr. Moon is Stoppard's only novel, published by Faber & Faber in 1967. It was not a commercial success.

The work is set in London's fashionable Mayfair and Westminster on the weekend England mourns the death of Sir Winston Churchill (1965) (though he is not mentioned by name). Lord Malquist, a bankrupt aristocrat, utterly disregards the realities of the world around him and lives the life of an amoral aesthete, using wit and charm to override everything that obstructs his baroque lifestyle. Mr. Moon is an unsuccessful man of letters, failing in his attempt to write his much-researched history of the world. He has hired himself out to write Lord Malquist's biography. Jesus on a donkey, two gunslinging cowboys, a murdered French maid, a free-roaming pet lion and eagle, sexually provocative wives, and fashionable 1960s London as a backdrop all surface in this highly unlikely tale, ultimately adding up to something sensible after all.

Enter a Free Man. Originally *A Walk on the Water*, this play premiered at St. Martin's Theatre, London, on March 28, 1968, starring Michael Hordern and directed by Frith Banbury. It played in New York in 1974.

In a working-class neighborhood, George Riley lives off the spare livelihood of his daughter Linda and matronly wife Persephone, spending his days in his room as an inventor. He is not a successful inventor, and most people see that fact. But his wife supports his dreams, and his pub mates tolerate his boastful but fragile confidence. George meets an entrepreneur, Harry, whom he thinks has bought into one of his inventions. Harry, however, is only humoring George as a harmless barroom distraction. Hopeful of this new opportunity, George decides to leave home to live with another pub acquaintance, Florence, and begin a new life. Wife and daughter humor him. He leaves, only to return when Florence turns out to be Harry's girl. Throughout the performance, the play is split into side-by-side domestic and pub-room sets to highlight the degrees of indulgence George receives from both worlds. The play ends with the dreamer ready to go through another cycle of dreaming, evasion, and denial.

The Real Inspector Hound. This one-act play was originally paired with Sean Patrick Vincent's *The Audition* at the Criterion, London, on June 17, 1968, directed by Robert Chetwyn. It opened in New York in 1972.

Two theatre critics, Moon and Birdboot, open the play sitting onstage waiting for a play to begin. They find themselves watching a conventional murder mystery set in the desolate Muldoon Manor. Moon is an envious junior staffer, and Birdboot is the type that uses his position to win the favors of aspiring actresses. In the murder mystery's second act, Moon and Birdboot are sucked into the play's action. Birdboot is shot and Moon is condemned for his murder, leaving a third-string reviewer to move up the ladder.

Neutral Ground, a television play written in 1965, was aired by Thames Television in December 1968, starring Patrick McGee and Nicholas Pennell, directed by Piers Haggard.

This spy thriller in the tradition of John le Carré is based very loosely on Sophocles' *Philoctetes* (about a warrior whom Odysseus must coax to return to battle in order for Greek victory). *Neutral Ground*, set in Eastern Europe, involves a double agent, Philo, who wants to retire from the business. British agent Acherson tries to bring Philo back to the British side. Much is made of the uncertainty that is central to espionage.

Where Are They Now? This 35-minute radio play aired January 28, 1970 on BBC's Schools Radio.

The play moves between 1945 and 1969. The latter time period involves the dinner gathering of a British public school (i.e., private school) class reunion of the boys who attended in 1945. The commentary involves the ways England's ruling classes are educated and socialized, as well as the matter of selective human memory.

After Magritte. This 40-minute one-act play was written for the Ambiance Lunch-Hour Theatre Club, London, premiering April 9, 1970, starring Clive Barker, Malcolm Ingram, and Prunella Scales, and directed by Geoffrey Reeves. It became a curtain raiser for *The Real Inspector Hound* in London and, in 1972, New York.

The play opens with an elderly woman lying on an ironing board, a younger woman in an evening gown on her hands and knees staring at the floor, and a bare-chested man in fishing waders blowing into an overhead lampshade. A policeman stares at the scene from outside, upstage. All is logically clarified for the audience as Inspector Foot interrupts and insists that this quirky trio was part of a reported robbery involving a one-legged minstrel wearing blackface. Each character recalls witnessing a different scenario, all unusual but plausible. The purported burglary turns out to be a misviewing of Inspector Foot himself having run from his own apartment with his wife's handbag in hand, hopping in his misfit pajama legs and carrying a parasol, all in order to plug the parking meter before it expired.

Dogg's Our Pet (one-act play, 1970) eventually became *Dogg's Hamlet*. See below.

Jumpers premiered on February 2, 1972 at the Old Vic, London, by the National Theatre, starring Michael Hordern and Diana Rigg, directed by Peter Wood, winning the *Evening Standard* and *Plays and Players* Best Play awards. It opened in New York in 1974, was revived in London in 1976 at the Lyttelton Theatre, directed by Peter Wood, and was revived again in 1985 at the Aldwych Theatre, by Peter Wood.

Dorothy Moore has recently retired from the musical stage, having lost her ability to remember lyrics and being disturbed by disorienting consequences of humans walking on the moon. As she haltingly sings during a celebratory party, the stage is taken over by a band of jumpers and tumblers, who turn out to be philosophers (who perform the same tricks with words). George Moore is in his study writing a lecture designed to prove the existence of god and moral absolutes. One of the jumpers is shot dead, and the jumpers' human pyramid collapses. This all occurs on the evening of a bloodless revolution leaving Radical-Liberal relativists in charge of governing England. Who shot the luckless jumper? Does god exist? Will Dottie ever be cured? Can ethical relativism work? George, insisting on moral absolutes, fails to help his wife, misinterprets evidence of all sorts, is outwitted by his servant Crouch, and miscommunicates with Inspector Bones. Meanwhile, on the moon two astronauts are fighting to board a damaged craft that can only safely return one of them to earth.

Artist Descending a Staircase. This radio play aired on BBC 3 on November 14, 1972, directed by John Tydeman. It was revised and given its first stage production in 1988.

Opening in the present with a tape recording of a man falling down a staircase to his death, an apparent murder, this play covers a span of fifty years and involves three artists. Its structure involves each scene slightly pre-dating the scene it follows until the midpoint of the play when a past-to-present chronology returns. Moving into the past reveals that Sophie, once sighted but now blind, loves one of the men for his art; after becoming blind she picks the wrong man, her real object of affection suffers silently in love, and she eventually commits suicide. The play includes discussions about art, reality, and truth. The last scene reveals that the opening scene was not a murder but an accident.

Travesties premiered in London at the Aldwych Theatre, by the Royal Shakespeare Company, on June 10, 1974, starring John Wood and John Hurt, directed by Peter Wood. It won the *Evening Standard* Award for Best Comedy. It opened in New York in 1975 and won the Tony Award and Drama Critics' Circle Award.

Henry Carr, a minor British diplomatic figure and wounded war veteran, reminisces about his time in Geneva, Switzerland, during the Great War. Tristan Tzara (a revolutionary "Dadaist" artist), James Joyce (the revolutionary literary giant) and Lenin (the revolutionary political giant), it turns out, all lived in the city at the same time, and Carr remembers being intertwined with all three men in one way or another. The play (initially entitled *Prism*) is filtered through Carr's memory and narrated by him, creating a lively but unreliable debate involving the nature of art, literature, politics, and their influences on the real world. Carr recalls playing the main role in a local production of Oscar

Wilde's *The Importance of Being Earnest*. The result is that virtually all of the action in *Travesties* is molded into a structure that recalls Wilde's masterpiece. What is fact and what is fiction ultimately reduces to the question of what is truth.

Three Men in a Boat. This adaptation of a Jerome K. Jerome novel aired on the BBC on December 15, 1975, starring Tim Curry.

Three friends decide to take a rowing trip up the Thames River in this lightly comic homage to Britain's pastoral countryside.

Dirty Linen and **New-Found-Land**. These plays began as an Ambiance Lunch-Hour Theatre Club Presentation at Inter-Action's Almost Free Theatre, April 6, 1976. On June 16, 1976 the plays transferred to the Arts Theatre, directed by Ed Berman.

This political farce involves a parliamentary committee assigned the job of investigating sexual misconduct among politicians while they are all in fact guilty of misconduct with the committee's secretary, Maddie Gotobed. Midway through the play, the committee temporarily adjourns, and two bureaucrats enter, reviewing foreign applications for British citizenship. This begins *New-Found-Land*. One of the bureaucrats breaks into an extended rhapsodic celebration of America. (The play was written for the American Ed Berman on the occasion of his attaining British citizenship.) The two men leave the room, and *Dirty Linen* continues, with the committee concluding no laws have been broken and no harm done.

Every Good Boy Deserves Favor. Music by André Previn. This "play for actors and orchestra" was given a single performance as part of the Queen's Silver Jubilee at London's Royal Festival Hall on July 1, 1977, starring Ian McKellen, John Wood, and Patrick Stewart, directed by Trevor Nunn, with the London Symphony Orchestra conducted by André Previn. It was revived with chamber orchestra in London, 1977, played in Washington, DC, in 1978, and opened in New York in 1979.

Two patients with the same name are placed in a cell in a Soviet insane asylum, one a political prisoner labeled insane for his convictions, and the other clearly insane, believing he is an orchestra conductor. The political prisoner has become a problem for the authorities since his cause has called international attention to the Soviet policy of declaring dissidents insane and locking them away. The authorities are willing to release him if he signs a document declaring himself "cured," which on principle he refuses to do. A senior official enters the cell to ask the one if he still hears orchestras in his head and the other if he still has dissident thoughts. Asking the wrong man each question, both men answer as expected and are released.

Professional Foul. This television play aired on BBC on September 24, 1977, directed by Michael Lindsay-Hogg. It won the 1977 British Critics' Award for best television drama.

Several Western European philosophy professors are invited to a conference on ethical behavior in an Eastern European country, site also of an important international soccer match. The soccer team commits a professional foul as the game is played, an act involving an illegal maneuver designed to prevent an opponent scoring. One philosopher, a fan, meets a former student, a native of this Eastern country who is being harassed by the authorities. Initially feeling that helping his student by breaking the country's laws would be unethical, the professor eventually reconsiders and does the wrong thing, which is the right thing, in essence a professional foul.

Night and Day premiered on November 8, 1978 at London's Phoenix Theatre, starring William Marlowe and Diana Rigg, directed by Peter Wood. It won the *Evening Standard* Award for Best Play. It opened in New York, November 1979, starring Maggie Smith.

Set in an unspecified African country shortly after liberation from British colonial rule, the country is now approaching civil war between an authoritarian government and a power-hungry opposition. The play is set in the home of a powerful British colonial businessman, and his wife is an attractive, intelligent woman bored by her life. Several European journalists converge on the house hoping to get a scoop on the unfolding political drama. What ensues is a debate about journalistic rights and privileges, free press in general, colonialism and its transgressions, and love and sex. In this realistic play, several dream sequences are included. All comes to a head when one of the journalists is reported killed and one of the journalists will miss his scoop because of a writers' strike back home which he ironically supported.

Undiscovered Country is an adaptation of Arthur Schnitzler's 1911 play *Das weite Land*. It premiered at the National Theatre, London, on June 20, 1979, starring Dorothy Tutin and John Wood, directed by Peter Wood.

A successful manufacturer, Friedrich Hofreiter, is living the good life, though friends around him seem to be committing suicide at an alarming rate. The play focuses on Friedrich's struggles to maintain order, especially when his wife is found to have cuckolded him in return for the many affairs he has had. The solution is to have a duel, at which time he kills his young rival, not out of jealousy but out of bored resignation.

Dogg's Hamlet, Cahoot's Macbeth. These two one-act plays were written for BARC: The British American Repertory Company, led by Ed Berman. They were first staged at the Arts Centre of the University of Warwick, Coventry, on May 21, 1979. On July 30, 1979 the plays opened at the Collegiate Theatre, London.

Playing with the Wittgensteinian idea that language is a game governed by rules, *Dogg's Hamlet* opens with "Dogg" language, intelligible English words arranged in a sequence that makes no apparent sense. One character learns to understand what the others are saying, confirming that there is a sense to the arrangements and definitions that they are using. The lighting changes and the "*15-minute Hamlet*" is performed (in intelligible English), a comic condensation of Shakespeare's play, further reduced to about three minutes in the encore. *Cahoot's Macbeth* follows, taking place in the living room of a flat in an Eastern Bloc city under totalitarian control. *Macbeth* is being performed when policemen enter to break up the gathering. Characters from *Dogg's Hamlet* eventually arrive, speaking Dogg and baffling the police inspector even as *Macbeth* has apparently done the same.

On the Razzle is an adaptation of Johann Nestroy's 1842 play *Einen Jux will er sich machen*. This free adaptation opened on September 1, 1981 at the Royal Lyceum Theatre, Edinburgh, as part of the Edinburgh International Festival. It premiered in London at the Lyttelton Theatre on September 22, 1981, starring Ray Brooks and Felicity Kendal, directed by Peter Wood.

A small-town grocer, Zangler, decides to spend the night in Vienna entertaining his big-city fiancée. His two youthful assistants decide to abandon their duties and go to Vienna as well. Zangler's niece is also sent to Vienna to live with her uncle's sister in order to move her beyond the reach of a poor but honest admirer, Sonders. The groups run into each other at various locales throughout the city, forcing them to ingenious devices to avoid being discovered. All ends well when it is revealed that Sonders is heir to a fortune. Everyone is paired up, and marriages ensue.

The Real Thing. Written for manager Michael Codron, the play opened at London's Strand Theatre in November 1982, starring Roger Rees and Felicity Kendal, directed by Peter Woods. It won the *Evening Standard* Award for Best Play. Its New York premiere was January 5, 1984 at the Plymouth Theater, starring Jeremy Irons and Glenn Close, directed by Mike Nichols. It won the Tony Award for Best Play, the New York Critics' Award for Best Foreign Play, the Drama Desk and Outer Circle awards.

The play opens with a scene of a husband catching his wife in a lie and trapping her into admitting having an affair. The scene, it turns out, is actually a dress rehearsal of a play written by Henry, acted out by his actress wife, Charlotte, and actor friend, Max. It turns out that Henry is actually having an affair with Max's wife, Annie. Max responds differently in real life than he did onstage. Eventually, Annie has another affair, betraying Henry with a young actor she meets on the set of the play *'Tis Pity She's a Whore*. The affair breaks Henry's heart, but there is reconciliation following a lengthy discussion about love and emotions. Annie has also gotten involved with a young man (Brodie) who has been imprisoned for committing political vandalism. She later discovers he committed the act not out of political conviction but merely to impress her. What is love? How do commitments work? What is "the real thing"?

The Dog It Was That Died. This radio play aired on BBC Radio 4 on December 9, 1982. It was also adapted for television and aired in January1989, starring Alan Bates, directed by Peter Wood.

Purvis, a double (triple?) agent, loses his bearings in life and attempts suicide by jumping off a bridge, only to land on a passing barge, crushing a dog sleeping on the deck. Having left a suicide note that identifies numerous troubling facts about the spy business, Purvis becomes a subject of keen interest. During his recovery, he is queried by his handler, Blair, about his life and his beliefs in the Western democratic way. Moving on to a convalescent home for recovering spies, it eventually becomes evident that the patients are running the place.

Squaring the Circle, Poland 1980–81. This work was televised in May 1984 on TVS with Richard Crenna as Narrator, directed by Mike Hodges.

This semi-documentary ("faction," a blend of fact and fiction) covers events in Poland from August 1980 – the beginning of Solidarity's campaign for workers' rights – to December 1981 – when General Jaruzelski cracked down on the human rights movement. Central to the idea of "squaring the circle" is the implicit assumption that trying to squeeze human rights into a totalitarian system is ultimately as unlikely (mathematically speaking) as it would be to square a circle. The play interweaves actual dialogue with imagined discussions, held together by the Narrator whose reliability remains suspect throughout.

Rough Crossing, an adaptation of Ferenc Molnár's 1924 play *Play at the Castle*, opened at the Lyttelton Theatre, London on October 30, 1984, directed by Peter Wood.

On the *S.S. Italian Castle* a wealthy band of actors, producers, composers, and writers is crossing the Atlantic to New York City with the intention of mounting a major musical. The composer overhears his fiancée actress involved in a romantic entanglement, which threatens to destroy everyone's professional plans. Ingeniously, the writer builds the liaison into the play, everyone insists the fiancée was merely rehearsing the revisions, and all is well.

Dalliance, an adaptation of Arthur Schnitzler's 1895 play *Liebelei*, opened at the Lyttelton Theatre on May 27, 1986, starring Stephen Moore and Tim Curry, directed by Peter Wood.

Fritz, a medical student and dragoon, is romantically involved with Christine while having an affair with a married woman. The events are mirrored in a staged Straus piece about an untrue soldier. When news arrives that Fritz has died in a duel, without ever bothering to confirm his love for Christine, Christine sinks into despair, sure to die herself some time soon.

Largo Desolato is an adaptation/translation of Václav Havel's 1985 play of the same name (Bristol, 1986).

A professor in a totalitarian country lives in fear because of his refusal to denounce his work.

Hapgood was presented by Michael Codron at the Aldwych Theatre, London, on March 8, 1988, starring Felicity Kendal, Nigel Hawthorne, and Roger Rees, directed by Peter Wood. Its US premiere was in Los Angeles at the Doolittle Theatre, April 12, 1989, directed by Peter Wood. Its New York premiere was at the Mitzi E. Newhouse Theater, Lincoln Center, on November 11, 1994, starring Stockard Channing and David Strathairn, directed by Jack O'Brien.

The play opens with a sequence in a London bathhouse: men walk in and out of stalls with and without briefcases as others look on. The onlookers are connected by walkie-talkies to a network of unseen operatives. Despite all attempts to follow the string of events, something "impossible" has occurred, and the observed sequence has left everyone scratching their heads. The scene turns out to involve spies and double spies. Hapgood is a British "mother," head of a spy network. Kerner is a scientist who is, or appears to be, working for her. He explains the opening scene by using quantum physics as his example, cases where particles can be in multiple places at the same time depending on who is looking and what one is looking for. At the moment, everyone is trying to find out who is leaking secrets to the Russians. Hapgood reveals the somehow coherent but incompatible nature of personal and professional behavior throughout the play, and she even performs her own twin in order to catch the actual twins who have been scamming everyone, including the folks who tried to follow the opening-scene sequence in the bathhouse.

In the Native State, a radio play, aired on BBC Radio 3 on April 21, 1991, starring Felicity Kendal, Sam Dastor, and Peggy Ashcroft, directed by John Tydeman. It won the Giles Cooper Award. It was rewritten for the stage and became *Indian Ink*. See below.

Arcadia opened at the Lyttelton Theatre, National Theatre, London, on April 13, 1993, starring Emma Fielding, Rufus Sewell, and Felicity Kendal, directed by Trevor Nunn. It won the *Evening Standard* Best Play of the Year Award and Lawrence Olivier/BBC Award for Best New Play. Its New York premiere was at the Vivian Beaumont Theater, Lincoln Center, August 23, 1995, starring Billy Crudup, Blair Brown, and Victor Barber, directed by Trevor Nunn. It won the Drama Critics' Circle Award. It was produced in Paris in 1998 at the Comédie-Française, making Stoppard the first living non-French playwright produced at that venue.

Set on an English country estate, alternating between 1809 and "today," the 1809 world involves an ingenious young Thomasina Coverley and her witty, urbane tutor Septimus Hodge in a debate about the nature of reality. Hodge preaches the standard, classical Newtonian version of reality, while Thomasina suspects an underlying reality that is more in line with the rising romantic spirit of her age, embracing uncertainty and irregularity even as her own surroundings (the estate) are being converted to the romantic landscaping style of irregularity, and even as the unseen romantic poet Lord Byron is apparently spending some time on site. The contemporary scene involves two scholars trying to recover the events of 1809, providing the opportunity for a discussion of chaos theory, which is a contemporary scientific equivalent of the irregularity uncovered by Thomasina in 1809. The discussions of reality entwine as the play's scenes entwine, leading to both periods becoming mirror (or "fractal") images of the other in the final scene, a dance that joins all characters and events together in a vignette of self-similarity that echoes the ideas put forth in the play.

Indian Ink is the stage adaptation of *In the Native State*, first performed at the Yvonne Arnaud Theatre, Guildford. Its London premiere was at the Aldwych Theatre, produced by Michael Codron, on February 27, 1995, starring Felicity Kendal and Art Malik, directed by Peter Wood. Its US premiere was at the American Conservatory Theater, San Francisco, on February 24, 1999, with Jean Stapleton and Art Malik, directed by Carey Perloff.

Set alternatingly in India in 1930 and in 1980s India and Britain, the play focuses on the (fictional) 1930s British literary celebrity Flora Crewe and an Indian painter, Nirad Das, who paints her portrait during her brief stay in his neighborhood. He initially paints Flora using European conventions but he eventually reveals his Indian roots by creating a second portrait. The interspersed 1980s scenes bring together the deceased Flora's now aged sister and Nirad's son, who is looking to unearth his father's past, as both try to avoid an annoying scholar's interventions. The two settings together add up to a discussion of colonialism and nativism, art and identity.

The Seagull, Stoppard's version of Chekhov's play, opened in May 1997 at London's Old Vic, starring Felicity Kendal and Michael Pennington, directed by Peter Hall. Its New York premiere was on August 12, 2001 at the Delacorte Theater, Central Park, with Philip Seymour Hoffman, Meryl Streep, Kevin Kline, and Natalie Portman, directed by Mike Nichols.

This translation reportedly "brings out" the play's comic dimensions.

The Invention of Love opened at the Cottesloe Theatre, National Theatre, London, on September 25, 1997, starring John Wood, Paul Rhys, and Michael Fitzgerald, directed by Richard Eyre. It won the *Evening Standard* Award for Best Play. Its US premiere was in San Francisco, January 14, 2000, at the American Conservatory Theater, starring James Cromwell and Jason Butler Harner, directed by Carey Perloff. The New York premiere was on March 29, 2001, starring Richard Easton and Robert Sean Leonard, both of whom won Tony Awards.

This play is about A. E. Housman, famed nineteenth-century Cambridge University Latin and Greek scholar, minor poet, and closet homosexual who chose a life of personal restraint rather than risky indulgence. Housman is played by two characters, the elder AEH, who reflects on his life as he is ferried by Charon across the River Styx to his final resting place, and Housman, who lives A. E. Housman's life through various stages, though he never fully experiences or consummates any real feelings of love. AEH comments and critiques throughout, eventually getting to debate with Oscar Wilde, the celebrated contemporary who gave all for love. Wilde has no regrets even among the ashes of infamy, while Housman is filled with regret even among the fruits of respectable success.

The Coast of Utopia. Part One: Voyage; Part Two: Shipwreck; Part Three: Salvage. This trilogy opened at the Olivier Auditorium of the National Theatre, London, during the 2002 season: *Voyage* opened on June 27, *Shipwreck* on July 8, and *Salvage* on July 19. It was directed by Trevor Nunn and starred John Carlyle, Douglas Henshall, and Stephen Dillane. Its New York premiere was at the Vivian Beaumont Theater, Lincoln Center: *Voyage* opened on November 27, 2006, *Shipwreck* on December 21, and *Salvage* on February 15, 2007. It starred Brian F. O'Byrne, Billy Crudup, Ethan Hawke, and Jennifer Ehle and was directed by Jack O'Brien. It won the Tony Award for Best Play.

The trilogy moves back and forth in time generating frequently overlapping scenes, and characters reappear throughout all three plays. Briefly:

Voyage is set in Tsarist Russia between summer 1833 and autumn 1841, mainly on the estates of the wealthy elite and intellectually curious who bemoan their condition as subjects of the Tsar and feel uncomfortable for profiting as serf owners. They debate political theory and consider the virtues and vices of Western European philosophy, especially German and French romantic rhetoric on love, freedom, and utopia. They rely on literature and journalism to change the world, debating the practical virtues of art as action and whether to emulate or reject Western civilization.

Shipwreck is set in Russia, Paris, Dresden, Nice, and elsewhere, from 1846 to 1852. Political activism turns to actual revolution as intellectuals work to mobilize the masses, only to realize that all their plans fail to prepare them for the realities of the world they thought they understood. Idealism is tarnished, and intellectualism is revealed to offer very little to the improvement of the world in general.

Salvage opens in a Russian exile's home in Hampstead, England in 1853 and ends in June 1862. It is a reflection of all that went well and poorly even as life continues. Activism continues and so do dreams. Persistence does lead to the emancipation of the serfs in 1861, but it comes without practical considerations like redistribution of the land. Karl Marx enters the picture, as does a new generation of radicals less convinced that words, debate, and good reasons will change the world.

Pirandello's Henry IV is a version by Stoppard commissioned by and premiered at the Donmoor Warehouse in April 2004, starring Ian McDiarmid and Francesca Annis, directed by Christopher Oram.

Rock'n'Roll opened on June 3, 2006 at the Jerwood Theatre Downstairs, Royal Court Theatre, London. Its New York premiere was at the Bernard B. Jacobs Theatre, November 4, 2007, starring Rufus Sewell and Sinéad Cusack.

The play is alternatively set in Cambridge, England and Prague, Czechoslovakia from summer 1968 to 1990, concentrating on events surrounding Czechoslovakia's Velvet Revolution. An unrepentant Marxist professor in Cambridge and exile from Czechoslovakia defends his position while attacking the extremes of the Czech government. His protégé, also a government informant, returns to Prague only to suffer the indignities of a police state even though his interests extend only to rock'n'roll music. In Cambridge there are sightings of Pan, the mischievous god of joy and disorder, who likely is Syd Barrett of Pink Floyd fame. In Czechoslovakia much is made of the Grateful-Dead-like band Plastic People of the Universe, who simply want to be allowed to perform their music, which turns out to be a threat to government control. Back in Cambridge there are idealistic debates on freedom declaring that Westerners have forgotten its value. However, newly liberated Eastern Europeans seem to sink to a similar yearning for capitalist profit, a tarnished outcome of the idealistic Velvet Revolution. The dream of personal profit, wealth, and fame wins the day, at the expense of higher ideals which have become all but forgotten.

Notes

Introduction

1 The name is pronounced with an emphasis on the second syllable: "Stop-hard."
2 Quoted in Jon Bradshaw, "Tom Stoppard, Nonstop. Word Games With a Hit Playwright," *New York* (January 10, 1977), 47–51.
3 Interview with Tom Stoppard by Maya Jaggi, *Guardian* (Sept. 6, 2008), n.p.
4 Stoppard repeats this story numerous times in various interviews and public lectures, including an April 1972 interview with Mel Gussow, collected in Gussow's *Conversations with Stoppard* (New York: Grove Press, 1995), 1–9 (see 7). Kenneth Tynan adds to the story in "Tom Stoppard," found in Tynan's *Show People* (New York: Simon and Schuster, 1979), 44–123 (see 45).
5 C. W. E. Bigsby, *Tom Stoppard* (London: Longman, 1976), quoted in Tynan, *Show People*, 61.
6 From a typed manuscript in the Tom Stoppard Collection, Box 121, Harry Ransom Center, University of Texas.
7 For a solid overview of Stoppard's film career, see Ira B. Nadel's "Stoppard and Film," in Katherine E. Kelly (ed.), *The Cambridge Companion to Tom Stoppard* (Cambridge University Press, 2001), 84–103.

1 Stoppard: briefly, a life in the theatre

1 Interview with Elizabeth Broderson (December 20, 1998), published in the ACT program for *Indian Ink*.
2 Stoppard's name is actually spelled Tomáš Sträussler, though Stoppard himself never uses diacritical marks.
3 Ronald Bryden, "Wyndy Excitements," *Observer* (August 29, 1966).
4 Ira Nadel reports that Stoppard's December 31, 1966 royalties statement records 481 home sales and 207 export sales. See Nadel, *Tom Stoppard: A Life* (New York: Palgrave Macmillan, 2002), 168.
5 In a congratulatory telegram to Stoppard dated June 10, 1974 (see Tom Stoppard Collection, Harry Ransom Center, Box 129.6) playwright Peter Shaffer jokes: "The number of good plays which you write seems to me to be considerably above the average which statistics have laid down for our guidance."

6 Connections between this early screenplay and some of Stoppard's later stage work are interesting. Consider, for example, that it includes an *Arcadia*-like carnal embrace in a gazebo and the kind of central female lead we will see in *Night and Day*. Space prevents full consideration of his screenplays, but there are quite a few fruitful connections worth pursuing.

7 Tynan, "Tom Stoppard," compares the work of Havel and Stoppard, demonstrating why Stoppard admired his embattled compatriot. See especially 73–82.

8 In a letter dated June 21, 1990 (Tom Stoppard Collection, Harry Ransom Center), Spielberg tells Stoppard: "Working with you is like working with the 7th cavalry – to the rescue at the last possible moment."

9 See "Rhyme and Reason," *Written By* (March 1999), 18–27.

10 Quoted in Tom Buckley, "At the Movies," *New York Times* (July 14, 1978), C-6.

11 From a December 1994 interview collected in Gussow, *Conversations with Stoppard*, 97.

2 Keys to Stoppard's theatre

1 See, for example, "The Event and the Text," in Jim Hunter, *About Stoppard: The Playwright and the Work* (London: Faber & Faber, 2005), 144.

2 John Gardner, *On Moral Fiction* (New York: Basic Books, 1978), 58–59.

3 See Victor L. Cahn, *Beyond Absurdity: The Plays of Tom Stoppard* (Rutherford, NJ: Fairleigh Dickinson University Press, 1979).

4 For a solid description of the theatre of the absurd, see Martin Esslin's book *The Theatre of the Absurd* (New York: Penguin, 1961), the source of the term, and Arnold Hinchliffe, *The Absurd* (London: Methuen, 1969), an excellent summary.

5 From an April 1972 interview collected in Gussow, *Conversations with Stoppard*, 5.

6 *Ibid.*, 3.

7 Stoppard, "Ambushes for the Audience: Towards a High Comedy of Ideas," *Theatre Quarterly*, **4** (1974), 6–7. Stoppard restates this infinite leap-frog point in numerous interviews and even gives the point to his character Moon in the novel *Lord Malquist and Mr. Moon*.

8 Kenneth Tynan, "Tom Stoppard," 47.

9 John Stead, interview with Tom Stoppard, *Evening Mail* (June 10, 1971), n.p.

10 Ross Wetzeon, "Tom Stoppard Eats Steak Tartare With Chocolate Sauce," *Village Voice* (November 10, 1975), n.p.

11 Neil Sammells, *Tom Stoppard: The Artist as Critic* (New York: Macmillan, 1988). Sammells's argument is an interesting one, but it becomes less convincing when applied to Stoppard's post-1980s theatre.

12 Katherine E. Kelly, *Tom Stoppard and the Craft of Comedy: Medium and Genre at Play* (Ann Arbor: University of Michigan Press, 1991), 3.

13 Jim Hunter, *Tom Stoppard's Plays* (New York: Grove Press, 1982), 16.

14 From a July–December 1983 conversation collected in Gussow, *Conversations with Stoppard*, 69.

15 Tynan, "Tom Stoppard," 49.
16 See, for example, Katherine E. Kelly and William W. Demastes, "The Playwright and the Professors: An Interview with Tom Stoppard," *South Central Review*, **11**.4 (Winter 1994), 5.
17 For more on this point, see Hersh Zeifman, "Tomfoolery: Tom Stoppard's Theatrical Puns," *Yearbook of English Studies*, **9** (1979), 204–20; repr. in Anthony Jenkins, *Critical Essays on Tom Stoppard* (Boston: G. K. Hall, 1990), 175–93. See especially pages 178–79.
18 Tom Stoppard, *Galileo*, in *Areté*, **11** (Spring/Summer 2003), 49.
19 Stoppard reports being influenced by James Gleick's *Chaos: Making a New Science* (New York: Penguin, 1988). For a discussion of Stoppard and chaos theory, see William W. Demastes, *Theatre of Chaos: Beyond Absurdism, Into Orderly Disorder* (New York: Cambridge University Press, 1998).
20 Clive James, "Count Zero Splits the Infinite," *Encounter*, **45** (November 1975), 68–76. A reprinted excerpt is in Jenkins, *Critical Essays on Tom Stoppard*, 27–34 (see especially 29–30), from which subsequent quotes are drawn.
21 From a December 1994 conversation, collected in Gussow, *Conversations with Stoppard*, 85.
22 From an April 1972 conversation, collected *ibid.*, 3.
23 From "Stoppard on Stoppard," in Hunter, *About Stoppard*, 125.
24 From an April 1974 interview, collected in Gussow, *Conversations with Stoppard*, 20.
25 *Ibid.*, 20.
26 From a July 1979 interview, collected in Gussow, *Conversations with Stoppard*, 35.
27 Sammells, *Tom Stoppard*, 15.
28 Stoppard, "Ambushes for the Audience," 7.
29 Contemporary consciousness theory has numerous models that look at consciousness in curious nonlinear, chaotic, quantum-mechanical ways. Much of what Stoppard does in his theatre actually parallels what contemporary science is proposing. Though Stoppard hasn't acknowledged any sources for his ideas (there may not, of course, be any sources to acknowledge), the reader may want to look at Roger Penrose, *The Emperor's New Mind* (Oxford University Press, 1989), Daniel Dennett, *Consciousness Explained* (Boston: Little Brown, 1991), and Antonio Damasio, *Descartes' Error: Emotion, Reason, and the Human Brain* (New York: G. P. Putnam's Sons, 1994). For an early discussion of the idea of consciousness in the theatre (including Stoppard's role), see William Demastes, *Staging Consciousness: Theater and the Materialization of Mind* (Ann Arbor: University of Michigan Press, 2002).
30 From a December 1994 interview, collected in Gussow, *Conversations with Stoppard*, 78.
31 Quoted in Alistair Macauley, "The Man Who Was Two Men," *Financial Times* (October 31, 1998), 17.
32 Quoted in Benedict Nightingale, "Catch-77," *New Statesman* (July 8, 1977), 62.
33 Tynan, "Tom Stoppard," 47, 56.
34 From a December 1994 interview, collected in Gussow, *Conversations with Stoppard*, 96.

35 Interview with Tom Stoppard by Maya Jaggi, *Guardian* (Sept. 6, 2008), n.p.

36 Tynan, "Tom Stoppard," 57.

37 Stoppard, "Ambushes for the Audience," 13.

38 Tynan, "Tom Stoppard," 100.

39 From an April 1974 interview, collected in Gussow, *Conversations with Stoppard*, 20–21.

40 In this case the source is Henry in *The Real Thing*, 32. See also the July–December 1983 interview in Gussow, *Conversations with Stoppard*, especially 40.

41 Stoppard, "Ambushes for the Audience," 12.

42 For a discussion of altruism, comedy, and *Jumpers*, see William W. Demastes, *Comedy Matters: From Shakespeare to Stoppard* (New York: Palgrave Macmillan, 2008), especially 116–24.

43 From a July–December 1983 interview, collected in Gussow, *Conversations with Stoppard*, 67.

3 The breakthrough years

1 Stoppard, "Ambushes for the Audience," 4.

2 *Ibid.*

3 *Ibid.*

4 Cahn, *Beyond Absurdity*, 33.

5 From a 1974 interview, in Gussow, *Conversations with Stoppard*, 35.

6 Susan Rusinko, *Tom Stoppard* (Boston: Twayne, 1986), 16.

7 Tynan, "Tom Stoppard," 61.

8 Kelly, *Tom Stoppard and the Craft of Comedy*, 67.

9 John Fleming, *Stoppard's Theatre: Finding Order Amid Chaos* (Austin: University of Texas Press, 2001), 36.

10 Tynan, "Tom Stoppard," 55.

11 Bryden, "Wyndy Excitements."

12 Tynan, "Tom Stoppard," 73.

13 *Ibid.*, 84.

14 Stoppard, "Ambushes for the Audience," 6, 16.

15 Robert Brustein, review of *Rosencrantz and Guildenstern are Dead*, *New Republic* (November 4, 1967), 25.

16 Curiously – and perhaps with tongue in cheek – Stoppard has said that these two Elizabethans "were always intended to be played by women. It has been a constant frustration to me that theatres persist in casting men" (Letter to two female students, dated 15/2/96, Tom Stoppard Collection, Harry Ransom Center, Box 109). But when given the chance to rectify the matter, Stoppard cast two men for his film version.

17 See, for example, Cahn, *Beyond Absurdity*, especially 35–66.

18 Felicia Hardison Londré, Tom Stoppard (New York: Frederick Ungar, 1981), 36.

19 Fleming, *Stoppard's Theatre*, 57.
20 Irving Wardle, "The Way He Tells Them," *Independent on Sunday* (March 28, 1992), 20–21.
21 Stoppard, "Ambushes for the Audience," 6.
22 Franc Smith, review of *Lord Malquist*, *Sunday Herald Traveler* (April 4, 1968).
23 Review of *Lord Malquist and Mr. Moon*, *Times* (March 10, 1968), n.p.
24 Kelly, *Tom Stoppard and the Craft of Comedy*, 24.
25 Rusinko, *Tom Stoppard*, 28.
26 Tynan, "Tom Stoppard," 55.
27 See, for example, Stoppard, "Ambushes for the Audience," 6–7.

4 Playing with the stage

 1 Stoppard, "Ambushes for the Audience," 8.
 2 *Ibid.*
 3 *Ibid.*
 4 Sammells, *Tom Stoppard*, 55.
 5 Paul Delaney (ed.), *Tom Stoppard in Converstion* (Ann Arbor: University of Michigan Press, 1997), 37.
 6 Stoppard, "Ambushes for the Audience," 8.
 7 This trauma stemming from the loss of a geocentric view of the cosmos is admittedly problematic, given that the issue arose during the European Renaissance. It is a stretch that must be conceded or a flaw that damages the play.
 8 A. J. Ayer, *Language, Truth, Logic*, 17th edn (London: Victor Gollancz, 1967), 88. Sammells, in *Tom Stoppard*, argues that George's lecture is "a protracted critique" (98) of Ayer's work, first published and widely acclaimed in 1936.
 9 "Seriousness Compromised by my Frivolity," in Gussow, *Conversations with Stoppard*, 15–16.
10 James, "Count Zero Splits the Infinite," 70.
11 Saint Sebastian's story actually has him survive execution by arrows only later to be clubbed to death. So while George very wittily suggests that arrows never actually struck the saint, the witticism involving death by fright doesn't quite work.
12 "Seriousness Compromised by my Frivolity," 14.
13 A. J. Ayer, "Love Among the Logical Positivists," *Sunday Times* (April 9, 1972), 16.
14 "What is Your Greatest Superstition?", in Gussow, *Conversations with Stoppard*, 29.
15 Hunter, *Tom Stoppard's Plays*, 240.
16 Paul Delaney, *Tom Stoppard: The Moral Vision of the Major Plays* (New York: St. Martin's Press, 1990), 64.
17 Stoppard originally considered calling the play *Prisms*, recalling, too, a Miss Prism in *The Importance of Being Earnest*.

18 To lighten matters, a French production famously had Cecily lecturing in the nude. Another matter further problematizes this scene, rather unintentionally, and led to a good deal of critical comment: it is presented unfiltered by Carr. In a 1993 reworking of the text, Stoppard has Carr silently remembering this episode just off centerstage as it is presented centerstage, preserving the point that the play occurs in Carr's head.

19 "Scoop" is an appropriate term, given that Stoppard was partly inspired by Evelyn Waugh's *Scoop*, a 1938 novel whose confused protagonist is named Boot.

20 "You Can't Help being What You Write," interview with Maya Juggi, *Guardian* (September 2008), n.p.

5 Science takes the stage

1 James, "Count Zero Splits the Infinite," 29.

2 See Kelly and Demastes, "The Playwright and the Professors" (especially 4) for Stoppard's insights concerning the writing process.

3 Kelly, *Tom Stoppard and the Craft of Comedy*, 152; refering to Richard Feynman, Robert B. Leighton, and Matthew Sands, *The Feynman Lectures on Physics*, 3 vols. (Reading, MA: Addison-Wesley, 1963).

4 James Gleick, *Chaos: Making A New Science* (New York: Viking, 1987). For a reference to Stoppard's acknowledged debt, see Kelly and Demastes, "The Playwright and the Professors," 5.

5 See Kelly and Demastes, "The Playwright and the Professors," 5.

6 Kirsten Shepherd-Barr's *Science of Stage: From Doctor Faustus to Copenhagen* (Princeton University Press, 2006) describes how "science plays" effectively move beyond mere theme and often experiment with science-influenced structures. Stoppard's two plays fall into this grouping quite nicely.

7 David Ansen, "Stoppard's Quantum Jumpers," *Newsweek* (April 24, 1989), 78.

8 Kelly, *Tom Stoppard and the Craft of Comedy*, 155.

9 The sentence comes from Richard Feynman, in *Lectures on Physics*, as Stoppard notes in *Hapgood* prior to the text of the play (vii).

10 In a 1998 note in a regional program for *Arcadia*, Stoppard notes: "Stowe, where two of my sons went to school, was naturally much in my mind during the writing of *Arcadia* … There was also Chatsworth, a bicycle ride from our first house in England. Here was the same in excelsis."

11 Benoit L. Mandelbrot, *The Fractal Geometry of Nature* (New York: W. H. Freeman, 1977), 1.

12 David Bohm and F. David Peat, *Science, Order and Creativity* (New York: Bantam, 1987), 183.

13 A discussion ensues about Lady Croom's interpretation of the Latin. The painting, by classical artist Nicolas Poussin (1594–1665), suggests that personified Death owns the words.

6 Love is in the air

1 "Happiness is equilibrium," in Gussow, *Conversations with Stoppard*, 41.
2 Anthony Jenkins, *The Theatre of Tom Stoppard* (Cambridge University Press, 1987), 159.
3 Toby Zinman, "*Travesties, Night and Day, The Real Thing*," in Kelly (ed.), *Cambridge Companion to Tom Stoppard*, 120–35 (130).
4 Fleming, *Stoppard's Theatre*, 165.
5 Letter from Tom Stoppard, dated January 31, 1995. Tom Stoppard Collection, Harry Ransom Center.
6 Fleming, *Stoppard's Theatre*, 212.
7 "I retain quite a nostalgia," in Gussow, *Conversations with Stoppard*, 124.
8 Interview with Elizabeth Broderson, published in the ACT program for *Indian Ink* (December 20, 1998).
9 *In the Native State* and *Indian Ink* are dedicated to Kendal and the memory of her mother, respectively.
10 Controversy arose on the film's release when it was reported that a 1941 novel, *No Bed for Bacon*, by Caryl Brahms and S. J. Simon, bore uncanny similarities to *Shakespeare in Love*. Stoppard admits to skimming the work along with countless other sources and offers the simple reply: "All the sources for information about Shakespeare are shared, so there are bound to be echoes and similarities" (Alun Palmer, "How *Shakespeare in Love* script swallowed a large slice of Bacon," *Mail on Sunday* [February 7, 1999]). Nothing apparently became of the claim. Shortly thereafter, a lawsuit was filed by Faye Kellerman, author of the novel *Quality of Mercy*, which was settled out of court for an amount suggesting the suit was unwarranted. As regards the collaboration itself, in a July 20, 1992 letter to Barry Isaacson, Stoppard indicates that his involvement was more than the term "collaboration" might suggest: "I have had to strip things back to the extent that I am using almost none of the original superstructure, and not much of the foundations, either" (Tom Stoppard Collection, Harry Ransom Center).
11 This is the scene from Norman's original screenplay that "hooked" Stoppard into joining the project. See Stoppard, "Rhyme and Reason."
12 *Ibid.*
13 Virginia was not settled until after Elizabeth's reign, a historical but minor error.
14 Though not designed as a comedy, the tragic undertones need to be downplayed. In a letter dated May 24, 2001, Stoppard observed that the play in production needs to be "less dark, more romantic – to be a success" (Tom Stoppard Collection, Harry Ransom Center).
15 Quoted in Macauley, "The Man Who Was Two Men," 17.
16 Quoted *ibid.*

7 Politics humanized

1 Tynan, "Tom Stoppard," 100.
2 Stoppard, "Ambushes for the Audience," 12.
3 Hunter, *About Stoppard*, 100.
4 Ben Brantley, "Young, Restless and Russian, Devouring Big Ideas," *New York Times* (November 28, 2006).
5 Hunter, *About Stoppard*, 104.
6 Brantley, "Young, Restless and Russian."
7 This success would be the envy of Stoppard's first great fantasist, Lord Malquist.
8 Michael Billington, review of *Rock'n'Roll, Guardian* (June 15, 2006).
9 Clive Barnes, "Czech It Out! Stoppard's a 'Rock' Star With His Latest," *New York Post* (November 5, 2007).

Conclusion

1 Enoch Brater, "Tom Stoppard's Brit/lit/crit," in Kelly (ed.), *Cambridge Companion to Tom Stoppard*, 212.
2 Personal correspondence, February 26, 2010.

Guide to further reading

Stoppard's creative publications

Note that there are multiple versions of most plays, and several are combined into anthologies. The following lists locate most of his published works.

Plays

After Magritte. In *The Real Inspector Hound and After Magritte*. New York: Grove Press, 1971. 61–105.

Albert's Bridge (1969). In *Albert's Bridge and Other Plays*. New York: Grove Press, 1977. 7–41.

Another Moon Called Earth (1983). In *Tom Stoppard: Plays Three*. London: Faber & Faber, 1998. 45–67.

Arcadia. London: Faber & Faber, 1993.

Artist Descending a Staircase (1973). London: Faber & Faber, 1988.

The Coast of Utopia, Part One: Voyage; Part Two: Shipwreck; Part Three: Salvage. New York: Grove Press, 2002.

Dirty Linen. In *Dirty Linen and New-Found-Land*. New York: Grove Press, 1976. 13–52, 67–73.

The Dog It Was That Died. In *The Dog It Was That Died and Other Plays*. London: Faber & Faber, 1983. 9–45.

Dogg's Hamlet, Cahoot's Macbeth. London: Samuel French, 1979.

Enter a Free Man (1968). New York: Grove Press, 1972.

Every Good Boy Deserves Favor. In *Every Good Boy Deserves Favor and Professional Foul*. New York: Grove Press, 1978. 11–37.

Hapgood. London: Faber & Faber, 1988.

If You're Glad I'll be Frank (1969). In *Albert's Bridge and Other Plays*. New York: Grove Press, 1977. 43–69.

In the Native State. London: Faber & Faber, 1991.

Indian Ink. London: Faber & Faber, 1995.

The Invention of Love. New York: Grove Press, 1997.

Jumpers. New York: Grove Press, 1972.

Neutral Ground (1983). In *Tom Stoppard: Plays Three*. London: Faber & Faber, 1998. 69–128.

New-Found-Land. In *Dirty Linen and New-Found-Land*. New York: Grove Press, 1976. 53–65.

Night and Day. New York: Grove Press, 1979.

Professional Foul. In *Every Good Boy Deserves Favor and Professional Foul*. New York: Grove Press, 1978. 39–93.

The Real Inspector Hound (1968). In *The Real Inspector Hound and After Magritte*. New York: Grove Press, 1971. 1–59.

The Real Thing (1982). London: Faber & Faber, 1984.

Rock'n'Roll. London: Faber & Faber, 2006.

Rosencrantz and Guildenstern are Dead. New York: Grove Press, 1967.

A Separate Peace (1969). In *Albert's Bridge and Other Plays*. New York: Grove Press, 1977. 141–74.

Squaring the Circle, Poland 1980–81 (1984). In *Tom Stoppard: Plays Three*. London: Faber & Faber, 1998. 187–264.

Teeth (1983). In *Tom Stoppard: Plays Three*. London: Faber & Faber, 1998. 23–44.

Travesties. New York: Grove Press, 1975.

Where Are They Now? (1973). In *Albert's Bridge and Other Plays*. New York: Grove Press, 1977. 117–39.

Novel

Lord Malquist and Mr. Moon (1966). New York: Grove Press, 2005.

Published filmscripts

Galileo. In *Areté*, 11 (Spring/Summer 2003).

Rosencrantz and Guildenstern are Dead: The Film. London: Faber & Faber, 1991.

Shakespeare in Love: A Screenplay (with Marc Norman). New York: Hyperion, 1997.

Translations and adaptations

Dalliance. In *Dalliance and Undiscovered Country by Tom Stoppard, Adapted from Arthur Schnitzler*. London: Faber & Faber, 1986. 1–53.

Largo Desolato. A Play by Václav Havel. English Version by Tom Stoppard. New York: Grove Press, 1985.

On the Razzle, adapted from Einen Jux will er sich machen by Johann Nestroy. In *Rough Crossing and On the Razzle*. London: Faber & Faber, 1985. 65–141.

Rough Crossing, adapted from Play at the Castle by Ferenc Molnár. In *Rough Crossing and On the Razzle*. London: Faber & Faber, 1985. 1–64.

Undiscovered Country. In *Dalliance and Undiscovered Country by Tom Stoppard, Adapted from Arthur Schnitzler*. London: Faber & Faber, 1986. 55–147.

Interviews

Stoppard has sat for hundreds of interviews. The following are two valuable collections.

Delaney, Paul (ed.). *Tom Stoppard in Conversation*. Ann Arbor: University of Michigan Press, 1997.
Gussow, Mel. *Conversations with Stoppard*. New York: Grove Press, 1995.

Selected full studies of Stoppard and his works

Though it is not an official biography, Ira Nadel's *Tom Stoppard: A Life*, listed below, is a detailed, very solid biography. For a firsthand account of Stoppard's early life, see "Ambushes for the Audience: Towards a High Comedy of Ideas," *Theatre Quarterly*, 14 (May–July 1974), 3–17. Kenneth Tynan's 1977 *New Yorker* article "Tom Stoppard," reprinted in Tynan's *Show People* (New York: Simon and Schuster, 1979), 44–123, is also quite good. No major works on Stoppard postdate John Fleming's book, listed below, which is both thorough and includes a full bibliography of primary and secondary materials.

Bigsby, C. W. E. *Tom Stoppard*. London: Longman, 1976.
Billington, Michael. *Stoppard The Playwright*. London: Methuen, 1987.
Cahn, Victor L. *Beyond Absurdity: The Plays of Tom Stoppard*. Rutherford, NJ: Fairleigh Dickinson University Press, 1979.
Corballis, Richard. *Stoppard: The Mystery and the Clockwork*. New York: Methuen, 1984.
Delaney, Paul. *Tom Stoppard: The Moral Vision of the Major Plays*. New York: St. Martin's Press, 1990.
Fleming, John. *Stoppard's Theatre: Finding Order Amid Chaos*. Austin: University of Texas Press, 2001.
Hunter, Jim. *About Stoppard: The Playwright and the Work*. London: Faber & Faber, 2005.
Tom Stoppard's Plays. New York: Grove Press, 1982.
Jenkins, Anthony. *The Theatre of Tom Stoppard*. Cambridge University Press, 1987.
Kelly, Katherine E. *Tom Stoppard and the Craft of Comedy: Medium and Genre at Play*. Ann Arbor: University of Michigan Press, 1991.
  (ed.). *The Cambridge Companion to Tom Stoppard*. Cambridge University Press, 2001.
Nadel, Ira. *Tom Stoppard: A Life*. New York: Palgrave Macmillan, 2002.
Sammells, Neil. *Tom Stoppard: The Artist as Critic*. New York: Macmillan, 1988.

Archival material

The serious Stoppardian would do well to visit the Tom Stoppard Collection at the Harry Ransom Humanities Center, Austin, Texas, official home to many of Stoppard's original manuscripts and professional correspondences. For a finding aid that details the holdings, go to www.hrc.utexas.edu.

Index

Cambridge Introductions to . . .

AUTHORS

Margaret Atwood Heidi Macpherson

Jane Austen Janet Todd

Samuel Beckett Ronan McDonald

Walter Benjamin David Ferris

Lord Byron Richard Lansdown

Chekhov James N. Loehlin

J. M. Coetzee Dominic Head

Samuel Taylor Coleridge John Worthen

Joseph Conrad John Peters

Jacques Derrida Leslie Hill

Charles Dickens Jon Mee

Emily Dickinson Wendy Martin

George Eliot Nancy Henry

T. S. Eliot John Xiros Cooper

William Faulkner Theresa M. Towner

F. Scott Fitzgerald Kirk Curnutt

Michel Foucault Lisa Downing

Robert Frost Robert Faggen

Gabriel Garcia Marquez Gerald Martin

Nathaniel Hawthorne Leland S. Person

Zora Neale Hurston Lovalerie King

James Joyce Eric Bulson

Thomas Mann Todd Kontje

Christopher Marlowe Tom Rutter

Herman Melville Kevin J. Hayes

Milton Stephen B. Dobranski

George Orwell John Rodden and John Rossi

Sylvia Plath Jo Gill

Edgar Allan Poe Benjamin F. Fisher

Ezra Pound Ira Nadel

Marcel Proust Adam Watt

Jean Rhys Elaine Savory

Edward Said Conor McCarthy

Shakespeare Emma Smith

Shakespeare's Comedies Penny Gay

Shakespeare's History Plays Warren Chernaik

Shakespeare's Poetry Michael Schoenfeldt

Shakespeare's Tragedies Janette Dillon

Tom Stoppard William W. Demastes

Harriet Beecher Stowe Sarah Robbins

Mark Twain Peter Messent

Edith Wharton Pamela Knights

Walt Whitman M. Jimmie Killingsworth

Virginia Woolf Jane Goldman

William Wordsworth Emma Mason

W. B. Yeats David Holdeman

TOPICS

American Literary Realism Phillip Barrish

The American Short Story Martin Scofield

Anglo-Saxon Literature Hugh Magennis

Comedy Eric Weitz

Creative Writing David Morley

Early English Theatre Janette Dillon

The Eighteenth-Century Novel April London

Eighteenth-Century Poetry John Sitter